10/24
STRAND PRICE
5.00

VERA WANG

VERA WANG ON WEDDINGS

HarperCollins books may be purchased for educational, business, or sales promotional use. For information address: Special Markets Department, HarperCollins Publishers Inc., 10 East 53rd Street, New York, NY 10022

FIRST EDITION

AUTHOR Vera Wang
CREATIVE DIRECTOR Polly Allen Mellen
ART AND DESIGN DIRECTOR Bridget de Socio
DESIGN FIRM Socio X

Library of Congress Cataloging-in-Publication Data has been applied for.

ISBN 0-68-816256-8
ISBN 0-06-008447-2, B&N edition

00 01 02 03 04 / 10 9 8 7 6 5 4 3 2 1

A SLIPCASED LIMITED EDITION OF THIS BOOK, SIGNED AND NUMBERED BY THE AUTHOR IS AVAILABLE: FOR MORE INFORMATION REGARDING THE AUTHOR OR COMPANY, PLEASE CONTACT VERA WANG MEDIA; A DIVISION OF V.E.W. LTD, 225 WEST 39TH STREET, NEW YORK, NY 10018, WWW.VERAWANG.COM

VERA WANG ON WEDDINGS

HarperResource

An Imprint of HarperCollinsPublishers

To my mother

VERA WANG ON WEDDINGS

FOREWORD

by Anna Wintour

It's been almost thirty years since I first met Vera Wang, in the offices of *Vogue*. She was Polly Mellen's assistant in the fashion department, and I, newly arrived from England, worked in a freelance capacity so obscure that I can remember only one thing about it: nobody spoke to me. Nobody, that is, except Vera. Vera was famously devoted to the magazine, and I sometimes suspected that she spent her nights at the office on Madison Avenue, perhaps nesting in a closet full of Saint Laurents and Sant'Angelos. She would have been perfectly happy. I don't think I've met anyone with a greater passion for fashion.

Or anyone, for that matter, with more determination. As a teenager, she excelled in the notoriously competitive world of figure skating, almost reaching Olympic standard. You'll read in Vera's tale of her own courtship how early romance was threatened by her future husband Arthur's one-track mind for golf. What you won't read is that Vera eventually concluded that if she was going to see anything of her husband on weekends, she would have to take up the game herself. Well, she's now an incredible golfer. This doesn't surprise me, because it's a sport suited to single-mindedness, a quality that Vera possesses to wonderful effect.

It's her work as a designer, of course, that is the greatest tribute to her resolution and adaptability. With no practical experience in the industry except her career at *Vogue,* Vera set out on a new direction in the high-stakes world of Seventh Avenue. Her first job was as a design director for Ralph Lauren. During her tenure there, she eventually became engaged. Her own experience of shopping for a wedding dress made her aware of a gap in the market for fashion-savvy bridal gowns: there was practically nothing available for the chic American fiancée in search of a modern dress. With that in mind, Vera became a designer of wedding gowns and opened her own shop on Madison Avenue. What she went on to prove was that a bride doesn't have to don corsets and ruffles and tiers of lace to walk down the aisle. It's possible to look fantastical but elegant, urbane but romantic.

With this book Vera Wang takes her brilliant instinct for bridal wear and applies it to every aspect of weddings. Only she could have produced such a beautiful volume of telling anecdotes, unforgettable photography and practical wisdom. I particularly love the way she classifies brides in accordance with their fashion personalities, so that a Sensualist is directed to an ivory pashmina and a Modernist to a Duchess satin pouf. Throughout she plunges fearlessly into the smallest nuptial detail. Should you splurge for hand-embroidered trims? Are pearls appropriate for tying the knot in the morning? How do you hide your tattoo? Should you provide party favors, and if so, how? Anyone who's ever had to think about getting married knows that this is exactly the level of specificity required.

In case it might be thought that my appreciation of Vera Wang on Weddings is purely academic, there's something I ought to reveal: it so happens that, for the last six months, I've been working with Vera on the wedding of my stepson, Joe. Every time Tina, the bride-to-be, is in New York for a fitting – she's from Minnesota and has to fly in specially – Vera is personally on hand, kindly and assiduously supervising every detail. (This is classic Vera: she's down-to-earth, unassuming and, as I learned all those years ago at *Vogue,* democratically enthusiastic about fashion.) With Tina, she asks – and answers – questions about every aspect of the big day: her goal is not to impose her taste or preferences on Tina but to help the bride realize her dream. This book will allow others to be so lucky.

Anna Wintour

While the thought of marriage can be all compelling, the headiest and most exciting part of a love story is always the proposal. That instant when you both just know. Whoever does the asking, the sheer thrill of being desired can be positively intoxicating, like the beginning of a new love affair, only this time with the added comfort and security of commitment.

Whether your proposal takes place over a candlelit dinner in Capri or during halftime at a Knick's game, you owe the magic of this interlude to each other first and foremost. It is important to experience your engagement as an ongoing process, part emotional and part rational. It takes endless amounts of love, patience and maturity to create a marriage. An engagement should be viewed as a valuable prelude to the rest of your life.

However long you've been together, the consent to wed will invariably raise new concerns. The resolution to many of these issues will also require compromise as well as time. The marriage you create can provide the love, honesty and compassion you both desire.

ON WEDDINGS

From me to you

For nearly two decades as a Vogue editor, fashion was my life. I had the unique privilege of collaborating with some of the world's most creative individuals. From styling the fashion pages to working with designers, I was in a rare position to communicate with women. I also learned to hone my eye and trust my creative instincts to an extent even I could never have imagined. The incomparable training I received continues to guide my work today.

As a fashion professional and a former bride, I am now able to translate all of that knowledge and love of style to the visual and emotional vocabulary of weddings. Having experienced weddings from both a personal and professional perspective, I can truthfully say that no one is more dedicated to brides than I am.

In writing this book, I was constantly amazed by the style, imagination and individuality of the women I've dressed. Not in my wildest dreams could I have anticipated the creativity my gowns would inspire and the impact of the clothes we so painstakingly create in our design studio. As photographs from all over the world started coming in to our office, I was equally moved by the beauty, grace and elegance of these celebrations. Each wedding represented its own unique take on a timeless tradition. From the gown and veil to the cake and flowers, seeing these brides in their moment of glory gave me a newfound appreciation for the work we do.

Each topic in this book is meant to be considered individually, as a practical guide to the ritual of weddings. It is also intended as a joyous celebration of women, marriage and style. Wherever you are in the planning of your wedding, this is my way of being there alongside you, for guidance and support or simply as a reference.

Ironically enough, as my husband so frequently reminds me, I never did manage to assemble our own wedding photos. For what it's worth, this book serves as my wedding album – as well as a thank-you to all the brides whose passion and spirit continue to inspire me.

My own two-year, two-part saga began when my husband, Arthur Becker, and I became informally engaged in 1988, during a trip to Hawaii. I can still recall every painful detail, since it was quite possibly one of the worst weeks of my life. We were having one of those difficult "romantic" holidays, like New Year's Eve, when people feel obliged to pretend they're having fun, because it's expected.

Looking back, I can see that Arthur and I went on vacation with two very different agendas. I had just left my longtime job at *Vogue* and was desirous of a brief respite from the frantic world of fashion. I envisioned long, relaxing moments with intimate lunches and walks. Arthur had his own passion. Unfortunately, it was for golf.

Having previously lived in Hawaii, Arthur was thrilled about getting back to the island's incredible golf courses. In hindsight, it now seems absurd. While I was picturing an intimate twosome, Arthur must have been planning foursomes with old golfing buddies. He was out every morning and gone for the rest of the day with only a "See you later. I have a golf game."

A TALE OF LOVE
From someone who's been there

Well, I didn't happen to have any old friends available, and the only obvious alternatives were to bake in the sun, surf or eat, with the emphasis on eat. Where was a spa, a gym or a specialty store when I needed one? Several bad novels and six miserable days later, I was feeling hurt, frustrated and lonely. Of course, on that particular day, Arthur finally stopped playing golf just long enough to take me to Kukuihaele, a tiny picturesque town high on the side of a volcano. That's when he blurted out, in spite of how upset we both were, or maybe because of it, "Do you want to get married?" That was my proposal. No bended knee. No ring. No nothing. Just angry Arthur and furious me on a hill in the middle of nowhere.

Even though this was not how I had envisioned my proposal would be, I said yes. And disappointed as I was that I had not gotten the proposal of my dreams, I loved him.

Our vacation made me realize that the blending of our lives was not going to be some quick dissolve to movie-like perfection. I was astonished by how different our needs and expectations were. It was going to take enormous work and compromise on both our parts to be able to create a life together.

Two years later, after what could politely be termed a long and drawn-out engagement, I finally got my formal proposal. And it was as sentimental and romantic as the one I had once longed for, and filled with just the right amount of hysteria. During dinner with close friends, Arthur arranged for my engagement ring to be placed in a piece of my favorite cake. As it didn't take long for me to eat dessert, Arthur immediately began to panic. As he leaned over to examine what was left on my plate, my eye caught a slight glimmer of metal. At that instant, I knew. Reaching over to hug him, I was genuinely filled with happiness and hope for what would be our future.

Here we are, guests at my best friend's wedding, July 1987, 8pm, Sag Harbor, New York. Little did I imagine then that our love affair would ultimately lead to the creation of this book.

IF THE ENGAGEMENT is a fait accompli, relating the news can be one of the most joyful parts of the wedding experience. The possibilities range from a formal announcement or dinner with family to a telephone call or e-mail to close friends. Happiness should be tempered with equal doses of sensitivity, candor and plain old common sense. Where children are concerned, they should always be informed first and in private.

THE TELLING

Who should be the first to know?

BEAR IN MIND that one's enthusiasm can be infectious, and sometimes those around the couple may be quite competitive as to who hears the news first. When telling people in tiers, it is only appropriate to ask them to delay in calling others until the bride has informed them herself. Even the sequence in which friends and family are told can lead to considerable resentment. Those who are the first to know should of course be invited to the wedding.

WHILE SOME COUPLES prefer to forgo a formal engagement announcement, others issue some sort of notice to the local paper. This is usually done around six weeks before the ceremony, to ensure adequate editorial space, particularly during high wedding season (May through September). In the end, a wedding invitation represents the ultimate engagement announcement.

A sprig of rosemary fastened to an invitation symbolizes remembrance.

THE ENGAGEMENT RING From solitaires, stackables and heirlooms to diamonds and precious stones of every conceivable cut and color, rings reflect the tastes and the personalities of the giver and the recipient. Unlike any other ring, however, an engagement ring embodies a promise and an unprecedented level of romantic expectation. It also symbolizes love.

BEFORE SHOPPING, all ideas related to size, style and budget should be addressed. Although a ring is not a prerequisite for making an engagement official, finding something that is treasured by both the bride and the groom is imperative. While there is no formal etiquette regarding the purchase, the notion that the groom spend the equivalent of two months' salary is antiquated by today's standards.

TRADITIONALLY, EVEN THOUGH THE GROOM has the task of selecting the engagement ring, a bride should still let her tastes be known. As couples today often prefer to collaborate on the choice of the ring, should it not be to her liking, the bride's response should be tactful and discreet.

ON RINGS

An enduring symbol of love

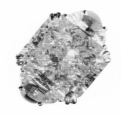

EVEN IF A BRIDE DOES NOT intend to wear her engagement ring on a daily basis, it should still complement the reality of her lifestyle. For those who anticipate wearing their engagement ring with their wedding band, the width of both bands should correspond to the size and shape of the stone as well as the proportions of the bride's finger. The rings should also be designed to be worn together. As with the style of the ring, the choice of the stone will impact how the ring will look on the bride's hand. In addition, the color of the stone should complement the bride's skin tone.

THINGS TO CONSIDER

THE FOUR C'S

Carat and clarity The Four C's are the traditional guidelines used to assess the quality of a stone. A carat is approximately one fifth of a gram. The size and location of inclusions — flaws — in a diamond determine its clarity rating. The amount of clarity ranges from flawless to most desirable, to imperfect. The fewer inclusions, the greater the quality and the value.

Cut and color A diamond's cut determines its brilliance; more facets, or surfaces, mean more sparkle. Color is determined on a scale from D — the highest — to Z — the lowest. The whiter the stone, the closer it is to a D rating. Subtle traces of color such as brown, yellow or gray are not desirable. These colors, however, are not to be confused with fancy diamonds, which are colored and extremely rare. If possible, the stone should always be appraised by the Gemological Institute of America.

A RING MAY BE ACQUIRED THROUGH
- A gem dealer
- An antique-jewelry dealer
- A jeweler
- A jewelry designer
- A specialty store
- A flea market
- An auction house
- One's family

Stones on skin: the color of a diamond is significant in terms of it's quality and how it enhances one's skin tone.

SHAPES ▪ A round diamond is the most traditional shape as well as the most popular. Due to its many facets, a round cut always catches the greatest amount of light. ▪ An oval shape is an elongated version of a round-cut diamond but far less common. ▪ An emerald cut stone is either rectangular or square. It's clean bold shape is extremely popular today with fashion-conscious brides. ▪ Pear cut is pointed on one end and round on the other, with the pointed end facing away from the body. ▪ The marquise is an elongated shape with symmetrical ends. It is not only more intricate but also more costly.

THE WEDDING BAND While an engagement ring signifies an intent to commit, the wedding ring fulfills that promise. Even though wedding rings do not necessarily validate a marriage, for symbolic reasons, they are usually exchanged by the couple during the ceremony. For many, a wedding ring represents comfort, dignity and a sense of identity.

IF FINANCES ARE A CONCERN, a delicate band of uniform stones could double as an engagement ring and a wedding band. Again, the color and finish of the metal should always enhance the stone. As with the engagement ring, yellow gold, white gold and platinum are still the most popular choices for rings and settings. Shades of gold, such as pink or green, can be original and expressive. Platinum, the hardest and most costly metal, is beautiful worn either on its own or as a setting for precious stones. All golds are available in 14-, 18- and 24-karat standards: the higher the karat assignment, the softer the metal.

THE RING PILLOW The actual wedding rings today are rarely attached to the ring pillow, yet the gesture of presenting the wedding bands at the altar endures as a modern wedding tradition.

A RING PILLOW, like everything else, should reflect the style of the ceremony, keeping in mind that simple is usually better. Although a pillow of any shape is suitable, my preference is a rectangle between eight and ten inches long and five to six inches wide. A ring pillow should never be too flat or overly stuffed. If possible, it could be coordinated with the fabric of the bride's gown.

PILLOWS EDGED WITH silk braid, velvet piping or ribbon always look subtle and refined, whereas elaborate hand-knotted tassels and passementeries are only appropriate for the most extravagant affairs. Some couples even have their names and the date of the ceremony embroidered as a commemorative detail. If there are two ring bearers, each one should carry a separate pillow.

ALTERNATIVES TO A RING PILLOW ▪ A Bible with a sprig of flowers ▪ An elegant monogrammed box of leather or rare wood ▪ For a country wedding, a tiny wicker basket lined in fabric.

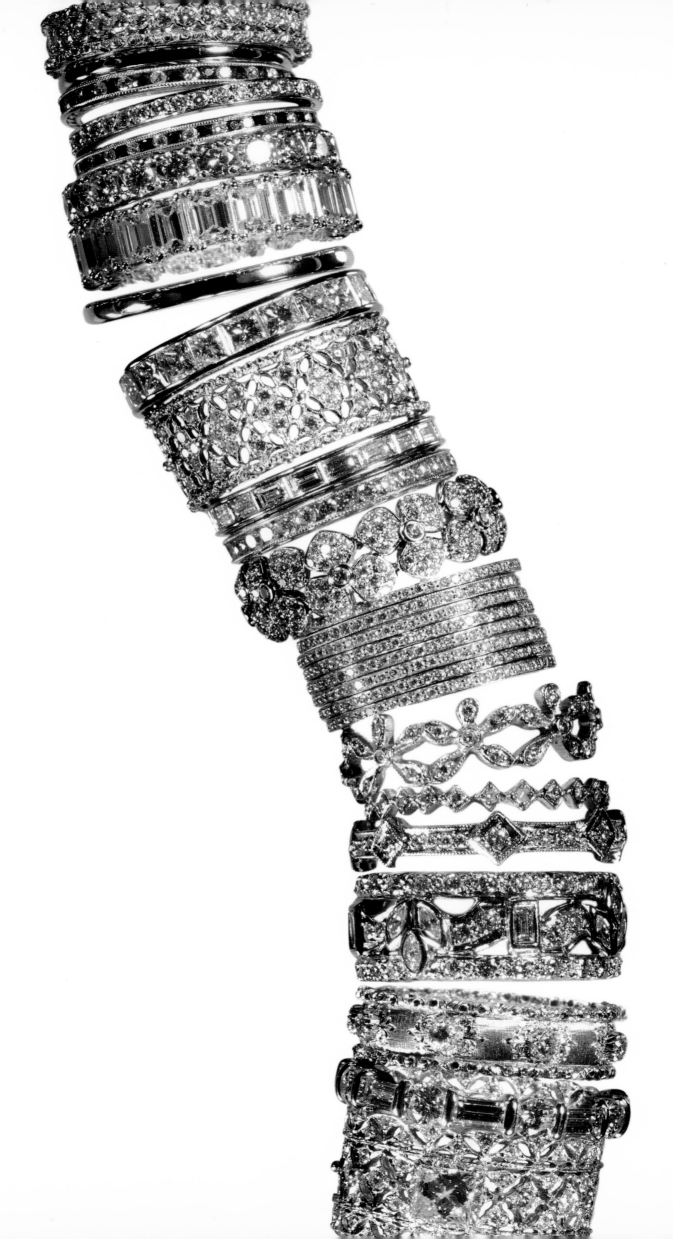

REGARDLESS OF HOW WELL a bride and groom know each other, the consent to marry is sure to expose new concerns. An engagement is a gradual process and one to which everyone brings a certain amount of personal history. At no time does this become more apparent than during the engagement period. TRADITIONALLY, AN ENGAGEMENT begins when a man asks a woman's father for permission to propose. This implies he is assuming full responsibility for her. As most women today are independent, an agreement to wed usually infers more of a celebratory importance than a proprietary one. FOR MANY, DESPITE their happiness, becoming engaged can imply a loss of freedom and, more significantly, identity. Learning to negotiate the delicate balance between autonomy and sharing one's life requires skill and compromise.

IDENTITY AND IDEOLOGY

The rules of engagement

NAMES It is surprising how much meaning is attached to a name. Some partners embrace the symbolism of name changing immediately, no matter who assumes what name. Others retain their maiden names or adhere to their professional ones. Some men even assume their wives' last name. Hyphenation is also a widely accepted way of safeguarding the identity of both individuals and families. In the end, any change of name represents a serious decision that requires great sensitivity and careful consideration.

IDENTITY AND RELIGION Some individuals wrestle with issues of identity well into a marriage. Even for those who are not particularly devout, a wedding raises fundamental questions of religion and beliefs. As many couples today may not be of the same faith, racial heritage or cultural background, it is essential that they communicate about these matters before wedding plans can proceed.

MONEY We bring our own history with money to the relationship. The subject of money can often translate into unexpressed emotions or an overwhelming need for control. While a prenuptial agreement need not revolve around a fortune, it does address issues of self-preservation, identity and mutual protection. For many partners, this may be a necessary part of the engagement process. In fact, to delay the resolution of this process until the wedding day can be extremely destructive.

A BRIDE SHOULD NEVER plan her wedding until all relevant financial issues are resolved. Adjusted levels of expectation and extreme doses of sensitivity should keep a couple, their engagement and the wedding plans on track.

AS LONG AS THE BRIDE AND GROOM are in agreement, any fiscal arrangement is acceptable today. For young couples, one side of the family is frequently in a better position to help with the wedding expenses.

WHEN DETERMINING A BUDGET, the number of guests and choice of venue will directly impact the overall cost. As most couples have a tendency to get swept up by the moment, they often lose track of budget. Fantasies are intriguing, but reality results in a far happier couple and a less stressful celebration. ▪ A daytime wedding will always be more cost-effective than an evening one. Most caterers, party planners and florists have greater flexibility regarding fees and available event dates for daytime celebrations. ▪ Choosing a date that falls in the off-season can also alleviate some of the expense and make scheduling easier.

OTHER BRIDES

SECOND-TIME BRIDES The concept of marriage has drastically changed in the last thirty years. Marriage is no longer a prerequisite for social acceptance, having children or rising professionally. People today get married because they want to. It is the fulfillment of a romantic ideal.

WHEN PEOPLE CHOOSE TO MARRY MORE THAN ONCE, they bring commitment as well as some practical experience to the decision. Second-time brides are often more excited than those who have never previously married. Sometimes women choose to renew their vows later in life with children and grandchildren and friends in tow.

WHATEVER THE BRIDE'S AGE OR HISTORY, there are few restrictions as to how she should dress. While most women usually opt for a sophisticated pale the second time around, white is always appropriate. And as always, the bridal attire is always determined by the hour, location and formality of the ceremony.

PREGNANT BRIDES Because of the different priorities involved, I love the challenge of designing gowns for women who are expecting. Since there is no way to predict exactly how a woman's figure will look, the style of her dress will depend on how far along she is and where she carries her weight.

MILITARY WEDDINGS Many young women officers choose to be married in uniform. I adore the importance and precision a dress uniform lends to a wedding. It is an emblem of pride and represents a commitment, the same way a wedding gown does.

SAME SEX The language of marriage has become much more inclusive in the last decade. Many young women choose to celebrate marriage to each other by wearing wedding gowns. As with every wedding, the dress should suit the occasion and complement the wearer. ▪ A couple should establish early on how they intend to live together during the marriage. Who lives where and who will pay for what are important questions to raise during the engagement. Adapting to the other person's lifestyle can be a big adjustment. ▪ If the lines of communication become blocked, it may be necessary to engage an unbiased third party to facilitate the discussion. ▪ Regarding all wedding documents, including the prenuptial, carefully read all documents prior to signing and sending.

FOR MOST BRIDES the very notion of white implies weddings. From the iciest shades of blue-white to the warmth and luxury of ivory, white remains an incredible source of inspiration for everything from the table linens to the gown. IT REQUIRES ENORMOUS confidence and style to wear white elegantly and effectively, and it is crucial to choose just the right shade for one's skin tone. While pure white can flatter a rosy complexion, warmer tones look best on a darker one. In winter, when natural light tends to be gray, ivories and off-whites enhance most women and lend an air of subtle sophistication to the gown.

ON WHITE

Inspiration comes in many shades

BECAUSE THERE ARE so many subtle variations, I am forever experimenting with white. Each season I create three new shades especially for my wedding gowns. For me, nothing is more enchanting than mixing several tones in one dress. Perhaps it is an ivory grosgrain ribbon on a white satin bodice or pure white lace on an ivory taffeta train. This deliberate blending oˆ whites has resulted in some of my most signature looks.

A FONDNESS FOR WHITE need not be limited to the gown. A veil, bouquet or wedding slipper can accentuate a white scheme, as can a floral centerpiece or an upholstered seat cushion. Due to its intrinsic purity, however, an all-white wedding requires enormous discipline. The scent of gardenias, the crispness of a white dinner napkin, the ceiling of a white tent or the glow of a white taper should all be meticulously staged to achieve a cohesive finish. DEPENDING ON THE BRIDE'S preferences and the overall design scheme, any tableau of whites can either be starkly minimal or decidedly elaborate. The marriage of different whites provides depth, dimension and texture without the distraction of color.

Left Full strapless silk zibeline dress with train, cut from one panel of fabric that knots in front, lifts over the hip and cascades down the back.

In ancient Egypt, brides wore gowns of white linen for good luck and fertility, while in Greece and Rome, white symbolized celebration. It was not until the wedding of Queen Victoria to Prince Albert in 1840 that white wedding gowns again became fashionable. Subsequently, every bride who wears white preserves the wedding tradition inspired by Queen Victoria.

ALTHOUGH MOST BRIDES regard white as the true color of weddings, many associate the joy of this day with luscious displays of color. Color speaks to each of us in different ways. Sophisticated pales, such as rose, celadon, sky blue or maize, can be flattering to wear, while elegant neutrals, such as gray, taupe, stone or nude, can bring a bit of subtle contrast to a bride's gown or her choice of décor. Intense brights, such as fuchsia, bougainvillea and periwinkle, always divert attention away from a plain venue or intensify the drama of a lavish celebration.

THE LANGUAGE OF COLOR

For the bride who dares

CERTAIN BRIDES choose to express their own sense of style and originality through the use of color, whether it is in the most minute detail or throughout the entire design scheme. Often an accent of strong color, like a piece of porcelain or a floral centerpiece, can alleviate the monotony of an all-white wedding. Conversely, a mélange of vivid shades may require some neutrals for balance. Color always provides an extraordinary canvas for the unconventional bride and the added opportunity to excite and amaze. ▪ Color sets the tone for any wedding. ▪ Color creates ambiance. ▪ Color should provide a becoming backdrop for guests. ▪ Creative lighting and flowers reinforce the presence of color.

FOR INSPIRATION ▪ In China, red and fuchsia represent the colors of marriage. ▪ In Ireland, green symbolizes fertility and good fortune. ▪ In Western culture, blue is symbolic of weddings.

Pale pink silk faille dress with dusty rose contrast stitching, side draped symmetrically over the hips. Cascade of Grand Prix and Black Beauty roses, with clusters of cytisus, jasmine and dianthus fastened to the gown.

In these photographs decorative lighting plays a seductive visual role in the overall design scheme. *Left* Vanessa Williams chose this sublime centerpiece as much for its fragrance as its visual beauty. The varied pinks of the roses and orchids highlight the dark tablecloth. *Below* I love the fuchsia clusters that were placed around the fountain at the wedding of Yvonne Force and Leo Villareal in Cuernavaca, Mexico. *Opposite* The drama of Sharon Stone's red lacquered living room was further heightened by the color of the roses on the mantels and in the urns.

DATE, TIME, CLIMATE, LOCATION

First and foremost

IN EASTERN WISDOM IT IS SAID THAT A JOURNEY OF 10,000 MILES BEGINS with a single step. When planning a wedding, the first step is setting the date, time and place. Everything hinges on these decisions, from the style of dress to the tone of the reception.

THE DATE Choosing a date involves many considerations. It may be a day with great sentimental value, like the anniversary of a first date, or the decision may depend on the availability of family and friends.

SOME GUIDELINES ▪ If the wedding is during "high season," from May through September, it is impossible to book too far in advance. ▪ If economizing is a concern, select a weekday between October and February. ▪ If the date coincides with a holiday weekend, expect higher rates from caterers and banquet managers. ▪ For summer weddings, a Thursday celebration avoids disrupting everyone's weekend. ▪ The date is only as important as the guests' availability.

THE TIME The time of day always determines the choice of dress and the style of the wedding.

Day or night, the presence of water provides an element of tranquility, while greenery in any form introduces the glory of nature to the celebration. *Above* Mr. and Mrs. Thomas F. Wessel, May 27, 2000, 10:30pm, St. Jean Cap Ferrat, France. *Opposite top left* Tanya and Stuart Lawson, September 2, 1995, 6pm, Fiesole, Italy. *Top right* Danette Alberico and Bobby Stuckey, May 6, 2000, 3pm, Sequoia Vineyards, Napa Valley, California. *Bottom* Alden and Emeril LaGasse, May 13, 2000, 6:30pm, New Orleans, Louisiana.

Morning Weddings Beginning anywhere from 11am to 1pm, morning weddings, more often than not, are about religious ceremony. They also epitomize a certain relaxed sophistication that frequently eludes bigger, more elaborate celebrations. Although filled with enormous religious pageantry, the morning ceremonies of Grace Kelly and Lady Diana Spencer were some of the most captivating weddings of the last century.

Afternoon or Late-Day Weddings Afternoon weddings usually start anywhere from noon on; late afternoon, from 4pm to 6pm. To my mind, afternoon or late-day weddings imply seduction and sensuality. From films to fantasy, literature to life, afternoons suggest moments of stolen passion and romantic urgency, they also inspire a special sense of celebration. An afternoon wedding affords the liberty of self-expression without the opulent trappings of some formal evening affairs.

Evening Weddings Beginning around 5pm, evening weddings can ignite great drama, grand gestures and extraordinary extravagance. Regardless of how religious the ceremony, the primary focus of most evening weddings is usually the reception. Nighttime weddings afford many brides the perfect excuse for lavish celebrations. They also present a wonderful occasion for an intimate gathering. Evening ceremonies are considerably more costly than daytime affairs.

THE CLIMATE After choosing the date and the hour of the ceremony, the next decision should relate to climate, as it will significantly affect the wedding attire and the ambiance. A SUMMER WEDDING in Aspen will differ greatly from one in Bermuda, while a winter wedding in Boston will be a decided contrast from one in Palm Beach.

THE LOCATION The choice of the wedding venue determines all of the basic planning. It will also affect the comfort level of your guests. While the location is significant in terms of menu, decoration and wardrobe, it may also impact issues of travel, lodging and transportation.

Whether you're furnishing a garden or tenting a walkway, the ceremony decoration depends on the climate and location. *Above top left* Jamie and Steve Tisch, October 9, 1996, 5pm, private vineyard, Napa Valley, California. *Center* Julie and Dan DeSerea, September 18, 2000, 4pm, Ghost Ranch, Abiquiu, New Mexico. *Bottom* Susan and Joe Werner, June 11, 1994, 5pm, Church of St. Michael and St. George, St. Louis, Missouri. *Opposite top left* Tanya and Stuart Lawson, Castello Vincigliata, Fiesole, Italy. *Top right* Melissa Barrett Rhodes and James Rhodes, October 5, 1996, 6pm, Brick Presbyterian Church, New York City. *Bottom* Cynthia and Dan Lufkin, June 24, 2000, 11:30am, St. Andrew's Dune Church, Southampton, New York. *Preceding pages clockwise from left to right* Courtnay and Brooks Haden, May 2, 1999, 6:30pm, Whilton Farm, Greenwood, Virginia. *Top right* Federated Church, Martha's Vineyard, Massachusetts. *Bottom* Hammersmith Farm, Newport, Rhode Island. *Right top* Jodi Della Femina and John Kim, July 8, 2000, 7pm, East Hampton, New York. *Center* A private residence, Martha's Vineyard, Massachusetts. *Bottom* The interior of the home where Courtnay and Brooks Haden were married.

A WEDDING INVITATION is usually the first decision a couple makes that so publicly reflects their tastes and the tenor of their wedding. At best, invitations should infer a sense of originality and imagination. At worst, they can look like a mere afterthought.

THE STATIONERY WARDROBE SHOULD INCLUDE ▪ Announcement cards ▪ "Save the Date" cards for guests who reside out of town or have inflexible schedules ▪ Wedding invitations and corresponding envelopes ▪ Response cards and their enclosures ▪ Other relevant stationery for maps, personal notes, possible rain dates or pew cards ▪ Invitations for prewedding celebrations, such as the engagement party, rehearsal dinner, luncheons, barbecues, cocktails, etc. They may be sent under separate cover or included with the wedding invitations. ▪ Escort table cards and envelopes for sit-down receptions ▪ Place cards and menu cards ▪ Wedding programs ▪ Thank-you notes and envelopes ▪ Gift cards for party favors or wedding mementos ▪ Wedding accessories that require monogramming, such as matchbooks, guest books or cocktail napkins ▪ Formal wedding announcements for those unable to attend or not on the guest list.

FOR THOSE NOT INVITED to the wedding, it is considered polite to send a formal announcement of the marriage the morning after the ceremony. The announcements should be prestamped, and preaddressed with the return address of the bride's parents.

THE WEDDING STATIONERY
The ultimate wedding announcement

FOR DECORATIVE EFFECT, a delicate grosgrain ribbon could be used as a binder. For less serious celebrations or an unusual wedding location, some rice, birdseed, seashells or confetti may be tossed into the envelopes. Uniformity of stamps always provides a nice visual cohesiveness to the stationery.
BE CURRENT AS TO ANY CHANGES in a guest's personal status. If a guest experiences a life-altering event, such as a divorce, a separation or a death in the family, these changes should be reflected in any correspondence.
AS ENGRAVED WEDDING INVITATIONS ARE COSTLY, handwritten invitations provide an elegant and personal alternative for a smaller wedding.
IN THE EVENT OF a cancellation, the retraction cards should be simple and, of course, all gifts returned.

THE GUEST BOOK Despite my best attempts to orchestrate our wedding, some details did fall through the cracks. One of them was our guest book. In the last-minute frenzy of our wedding, not one of our ushers remembered to have guests sign in. We were disappointed that the words we would have treasured were never recorded. While videos and photographs convey a sense of immediacy, handwritten notes are irreplaceable.

▪ Make sure the guest book is in a convenient and obvious location. ▪ Designate someone to have guests sign in and to retrieve the guest book after the ceremony. ▪ For a large wedding, more than one book and several pens should be made available to guests. ▪ All addresses in the guest book should be printed for legibility, in case the master list is incorrect. Guests should print and sign their names. ▪ If need be, the guest book should be displayed at the reception so guests can sign throughout the duration. ▪ Sometimes a couple may provide cards and envelopes for guests to write a more personal message. ▪ For a decorative touch, have the guest books monogrammed.

SOME MORE GENERAL GUIDELINES ▪ Invitations should be ordered only after the number of guests has been approximated. ▪ To avoid any unforeseen disasters, all stationery should be ordered at least three months prior to the wedding, especially if it takes place during high season. ▪ For uniformity, all wedding stationery should be ordered at the same time.

Herr und Frau Dr. Dieter Frank Kastler

laden herzlich ein zur Trauung

ihrer Tochter

Maja Angela Sieglinde

mit

Nicholas Paepcke DuBrul

im Samstag den 17. Juni 1995

um 14.00 Uhr

Mr. and Mrs. Johnson Robert Go

request the honour of your presence

at the marriage of their daughter

Vanessa

to

Brian Edward Murfin

Saturday, the second of September

the year Two thousand

at four o'clock

Church of the Blessed Sacrament

Reception
following the ceremony
Duck Pond Road
Locust Valley

Barnett
presence
daughter
rnett

yles
nth of June

Nineteen hundred and ninety-six

at half after five o'clock

Saint John's Church

Cold Spring Harbor

N. Y.

CMR

Mrs. Kerstin Viola Jamison

Mr. Frank Leighton Jamison

Mr. and Mrs. William Lawrence Mack

request the honour of your presence

at the marriage of

Christine Marie Jamison

to

Mr. Richard Jay Mack

Saturday, the seventeenth of January

Nineteen hundred and ninety-eight

at half after seven o'clock

The Waldorf Astoria

New York

Black tie

Mrs. Leslie Gaillard Cline

Mr. Michael James Collins

request the honour of your presence

at the marriage of their daughter

Catherine Elise

to

Mr. George McLaughlin Masterson

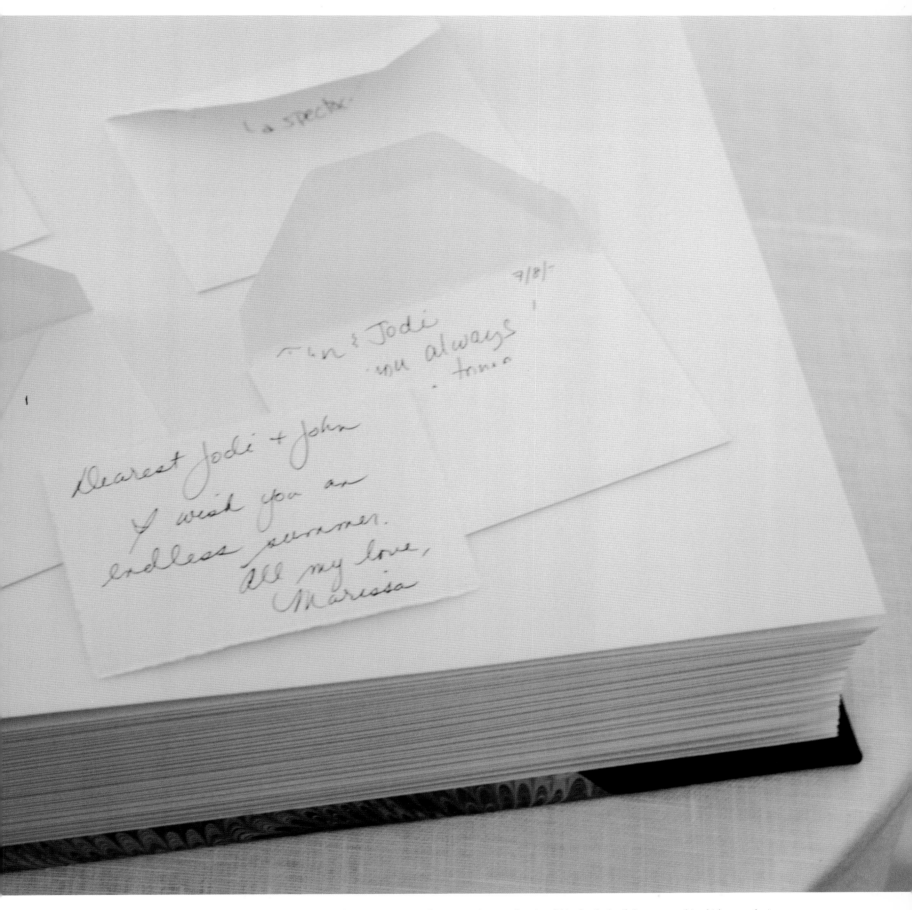

Wedding invitations require many serious decisions concerning fonts, engraving or embossing, folds, the shade of the paper, and its thickness and trim.

THE WEDDING SERVICE The specifics of any wedding ceremony can vary enormously, depending upon one's religious beliefs or preferences. If the service is to be written and delivered by the couple, the content should be kept personal, relevant and concise. As no ceremony should ever become tedious, the shorter and more heartfelt the service, the more pleasurable the wedding. A LENGTHY CEREMONY can even have serious physical repercussions for some of those present. Individuals in perfect health could find standing upright for more than an hour to be a significant challenge. My brother, Ken, once fainted during an interminable Greek Orthodox ceremony. CLIMATE CONTROL is an important consideration, too. So is overcrowding and poor ventilation. Street sounds, sirens and alarms or other unintended noise, can be as distracting as they are irritating. Nothing should prevent the guests from focusing their attention on the service.

Printing the couple's name on the ribbon binder is an elegant way to personalize the wedding program.

THE CEREMONY

The glorification of commitment

WHILE MANY religions have strict rules regarding weddings of mixed faiths, there are suitable and qualified officiants willing and able to conduct interfaith ceremonies. The bride and groom should make a deliberate effort to get to know their officiant before the wedding ceremony, as nothing is more disingenuous than an impersonal service. SINCE MARRIAGE concerns culture and religion equally, it is extremely important to be sensitive to the feelings and spiritual beliefs of both families.

THE PROGRAM Many couples choose to commemorate their wedding ceremony with a special program. Like the invitation, a program should reflect the style of the ceremony and the personal tastes of the bride and groom. It should also designate the names of the participants, the order of the service and the musical selections. A ceremony program always provides a personal and stylish way of welcoming guests and acknowledging the wedding party.

- If permissible, have each guest hold a lit candle during the ceremony.
- For a Jewish service, the yarmulkes should be placed clearly in view.
- For a more inclusive wedding service, family members or close friends could read a special poetry selection or perform a piece of music.

THE CEREMONY DECORATION

The spiritual implications of it all

FROM THE AISLE TO THE ALTAR, the ceremony decoration should emphasize the spiritual portion of the wedding and the beauty of the service. DUE TO THE RANGE IN STYLES AND VENUES, the entire context of ceremony decoration now assumes a whole other level of significance. From a giant shade tree for an altar to the Pacific Ocean as a backdrop, from a lavish floral arbor to the splendor of the Sistine Chapel, the possibilities for staging a ceremony are limitless.

THE CEREMONY FLOWERS Few things are more closely associated with weddings than fresh flowers. Their vibrant beauty captivates the eye and celebrates the occasion. Too often, however, their delicate fragrance is overlooked in favor of their visual importance. Unless there is an overabundance of scented flowers, particularly in a grand venue, their perfume may be barely perceptible.

DUE TO THE EXPENSE, some couples choose to forgo ceremony flowers altogether, preferring to focus their resources on the reception.

Above and opposite The splendor and majesty of two very different chuppahs. Garlands of colorful blossoms, leaves and hanging moss adorn the incredible outdoor chuppah at Jamie and Steve Tisch's California wedding. *Opposite* Opulent swags of white georgette fastened with extravagant bouquets of white roses characterize an indoor chuppah of great beauty and femininity for the wedding of Mr. and Mrs. William J. Diggins III, March 16, 1996, 7pm, The Plaza Hotel, New York City. *Top* Hand-rolled individual programs were carefully fashioned into a delicate chain of ribbon decorated with wisps of pink organdy at each end for the wedding of Jamie and Steve Tisch.

▪ Decorating with candles provides an effective and far less costly design alternative to flowers. ▪ Even if the ceremony does not take place in a traditional house of worship, a couple may wish to simulate the floor plan of a religious venue. Pairs of rented trees, candelabra or velvet ropes can all serve to delineate an aisle. ▪ For a limited budget, flowers should be used only at the altar or chuppah. ▪ Certain churches or synagogues are so awe-inspiring, even the most minimal decoration may feel like an unwelcome distraction. ▪ No matter how enchanting the surroundings or panoramic the view, weather is always a consideration at an outdoor wedding.

THE CEREMONY SEATING While the staging of a ceremony in a church or synagogue predetermines most issues of seating, other more secular venues may present their own serious logistical and design challenges. Even though all the activity at a wedding ceremony centers around the aisle and the altar, it also involves the seating.

▪ The decorative possibilities might include an arrangement on each pew, or garlands of flowers, silk ropes or pairs of candelabra along both sides of the aisle. ▪ For alternative ceremony venues, such as a tent, a country club or a private home, positioning the chairs in a more unusual formation, such as a cross, a circle or at an angle, adds significant design interest. ▪ Depending on the location and the number of guests, and if rental chairs are required, chairs should be chosen for their overall visual appeal. Make them more comfortable and stylish with padded slipcovers or special seat cushions. ▪ A silk ribbon along the length of each row or simple bows fastened to the back of each chair can provide additional decorative interest. So can a program attached to each seat. ▪ Rose petals scattered across each seat add fragrance, whimsy and visual charm. ▪ For extremely warm weather, provide elegant paper fans. ▪ Ample room should be provided for older or disabled guests. ▪ In order to fully participate in the proceedings, every guest should be comfortably seated within hearing distance and with an unobstructed view of the aisle and altar.

Rows of long pine benches in a rustic country barn, French bistro chairs in a Medieval cloister and scattered lawn chairs in a gravel garden facing a vineyard are all wonderfully imaginative seating possibilities for a wedding service. *Left* As per Tuscan wedding tradition, Tanya Lawson decorated a giant stone bird bath with bouquets of laurel leaves and lemons. *Opposite* An enormous sprawling oak tree provides a unique focal point for a romantic outdoor wedding ceremony, Fieldstone Winery and Vineyard, Healdsberg, California.

THE AISLE Whether it's a walk down a narrow path to the beach or a procession through the center of St. Paul's Cathedral, the ceremonial aisle represents the ultimate stage for the bride's most triumphant moment. ▪ The longer the aisle, the more formal the ceremony. ▪ The width of the aisle and runner may present logistical concerns for a voluminous gown or attendants walking double file. ▪ Nothing looks worse than a skimpy runner except a crooked one. ▪ Traditionally, the unfurling of the runner is the task of two designated ushers. ▪ Make certain that the runner lies flat on the floor. Safety should always be a top priority. ▪ The runner should also be secured with "no-slip" padding. ▪ If possible, coordinate the runner to accentuate or complement the gown. A pure white runner can make an ivory gown appear dingy, while an ornate runner, however fanciful, could clash with generic hotel carpeting. ▪ If adorning the aisle with strewn petals, make certain that everyone, particularly the bride, proceeds with caution.

THE ALTAR An altar represents a sanctuary of great religious, emotional and historic consequence. In the Jewish faith, a chuppah represents the house into which the bride and groom both enter. The roof of the chuppah is meant to symbolize the roof over their heads. Many couples go to enormous effort and much expense to create a chuppah of exceptional beauty and dignity. IF PERMISSIBLE, an altar may be elaborately adorned with fresh flowers and candles. For more secular ceremonies, many couples choose to create a symbolic altar as a focal point for the wedding service. Whether it is a giant urn filled with branches, a towering shade tree, an elaborate sand castle or a monumental fireplace, the altar always assumes a sacred significance.

Top left The wooden pews at Vanessa Williams' church wedding were lavishly adorned with ivory candles and sophisticated topiaries of magnolia leaves and white roses, September 26, 1999, 3pm, The Church of the Holy Trinity, New York City. *Middle left* An extravagant floral arbor was brilliantly conceived to cover the aisle for the bride and guests to walk beneath at Mara Leighton and Scott Weiner's winter wedding, December 5, 1998, 7pm, The Pierre Hotel, New York City. *Bottom left* I adore the splendor and dignity of Chynna Phillips and William Baldwin's summer candlelight wedding service, September 9, 1995, 1:30pm. *Opposite* There's something so incredibly enchanting about blue wedding ribbons festooned across a wedding aisle covered with rose petals. A simple stone urn filled with fresh white flowers and ivy substitutes for a traditional altar, Annadel Winery and Gardens, Sonoma Valley, California.

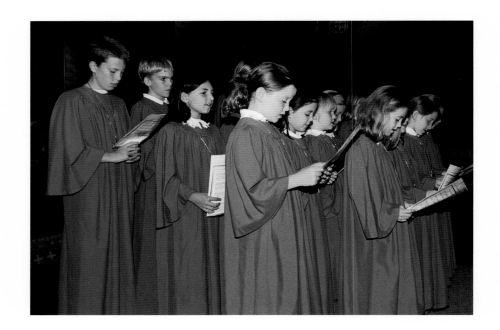

Right A children's choir serenades Cynthia and Dan Lufkin at their seaside ceremony, St. Andrew's Dune Church, Southampton, New York. *Middle* I love the festive touch of musicians in traditional Scottish dress. Julie and Donald Munro, September 9, 1993, 5:30pm, East Hampton, New York. *Bottom* The Empire String Quartet from The Juilliard School of Music provides the perfect accompaniment of classical music, The Georgian Suite, New York City.

THE CEREMONY MUSIC
The glorious sound of anticipation

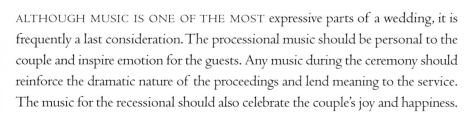

ALTHOUGH MUSIC IS ONE OF THE MOST expressive parts of a wedding, it is frequently a last consideration. The processional music should be personal to the couple and inspire emotion for the guests. Any music during the ceremony should reinforce the dramatic nature of the proceedings and lend meaning to the service. The music for the recessional should also celebrate the couple's joy and happiness.

■ The choice of music affects everything else. ■ Music always enhances the mood of the ceremony. ■ Many couples choose different pieces of music for each group in the processional. ■ The choice of music need not always be classical. Poignant renditions of popular songs are every bit as moving as a string quartet. ■ The musical possibilities for a ceremony can range from a children's choir, a church organist or a chamber music group to a cantor or soloist.

MUSICAL SUGGESTIONS
"Canon in D," by Johann Pachelbel
"Trumpet Voluntary" ("Prince of Denmark's March"), by Jeremiah Clarke
"Romanza," from *Eine kleine Nachtmusik*, by Wolfgang Amadeus Mozart
"Bridal Chorus" ("Here Comes the Bride") from *Lohengrin*, by Richard Wagner
"Anglaise Minuet for Hornpipe," by George Frideric Handel
"Heroic Music," by Georg Phillipp Telemann
"Fifth Movement," *Sonata Tromba*, by Arcangelo Corelli
"Rondeau," from *Fanfares avec une Suite de Simphonies*, by Jean-Joseph Mouret
"Jesu, Joy of Man's Desiring," Cantata #147, by Johann Sebastian Bach
"Wedding March," from *A Midsummer Night's Dream*, by Felix Mendelssohn
"Spring," from *The Four Seasons*, by Antonio Vivaldi
"Arrival of the Queen of Sheba," from *Solomon*, by George Frideric Handel
"Marche Gay," from *Symphonies for the King's Bed Chamber*, by Jean-Baptiste Lully
"The Trumpet Shall Sound," from *The Messiah*, by George Frideric Handel

The Wedding Party
James Driscoll
John Driscoll
Justine Harari
Nicholas Loeb
Elise Paschen
Amanda Weil

The Ushers
Stephen Corridan
Edward Conlon
Edward Kennedy, Jr.
John Lambros
Jeffrey Leeds
Michael Mailer
David Nunes
Scott Patton
Kevin Ward

The Gentlemen of the St. Thomas Choir
Peter Stoltzfus, Assistant Organist, Director of the Choir
R. Wesley McAfee, Assisting Organist

ORDER OF SERVICE

ORGAN PRELUDE

AT THE PROCESSION

Prelude to a Te Deum   Marc Antoine Charpentier
(1634-1704)

The Prince of Denmark's March   Jeremiah Clarke
(1674-1707)

THE EXHORTATION

THE DECLARATION OF CONSENT

THE SALUTATION AND COLLECT

Officiant   The Lord be with you.
People   And with thy spirit.
Officiant   Let us pray. (The Officiant says the Colle
People   Amen.

THE O   LESSON

The S   f Solom   2

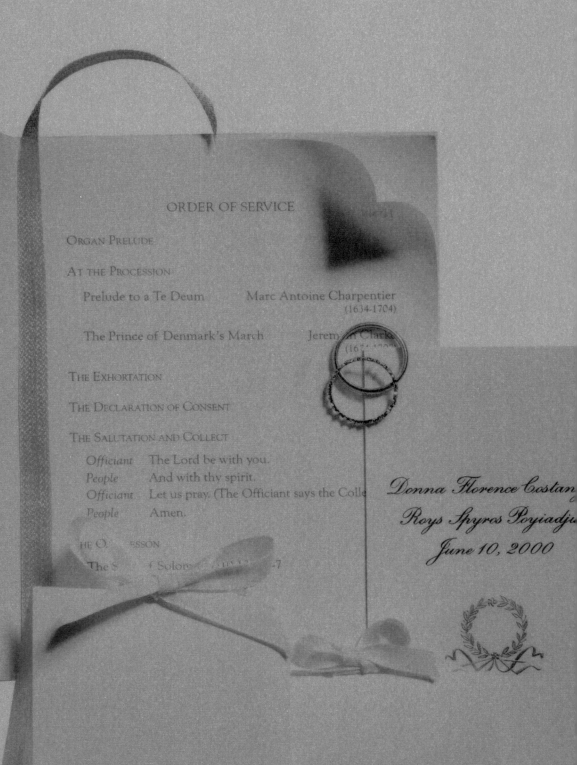

Donna Florence Costan
Roys Spyros Poyiadju
June 10, 2000

$\mathcal{DCR}$

L · A

THE WEDDING PROCESSIONAL REPRESENTS the bride's most defining moment. After all the months of planning, a sense of anticipation is nearly palpable as she begins her symbolic journey down the aisle. All the bride's attendants contribute to the excitement of her arrival and to the enormous significance of such an important rite of passage. The wedding processional should always be staged to maximize the theatrical nature of the proceedings.

THE PROCESSIONAL

The desire to enchant, the power to inspire

■ To personalize the processional, have each attendant carry different flowers or commemorative objects such as ceremonial candles. ■ Any variation on the sequence of the processional can add an element of surprise. ■ Music should capture the mystery and the majesty of the ceremony. ■ Even by day, candlelight always creates beauty, reverence and atmosphere. ■ The order of the processional is likely to vary depending upon the denomination of the service.

FOR A CHRISTIAN WEDDING, the minister, groom and best man enter from the side and face the processional. The mother of the bride is usually escorted by a male member of the family and then seated, before the processional begins. The march down the aisle is led by the groomsmen, followed by the bride's attendants, the flower girl, the ring bearer and, lastly, the maid of honor. The bride is always accompanied by her father or another designated member of the family.

FOR A TRADITIONAL JEWISH WEDDING, the rabbi and cantor lead the processional. They are followed by the grandparents of the bride, the grandparents of the groom, all of the ushers and the best man. The groom is accompanied by both of his parents as he proceeds down the aisle. The bridesmaids and the maid of honor are next and directly precede the bride. She, too, is accompanied by both her mother and father. The men always walk to the left and the women to the right.

Top For her New York City church wedding, Melissa Barrett Rhodes wears a long, gathered, pouf veil with a traditional shoulder-length blusher. *Opposite* Christine Mack opts for the sensuality and drama of a dropped cathedral veil to be worn over a wedding train of equal length. *Left* For her wedding at La Maison Opéra in Paris, Philippa Feigen Malkin prefers the originality of a fingertip blusher with a chapel length veil. She is escorted by her father, renowned art dealer, Richard L. Feigen.

THE RECESSIONAL

A tribute to the couple

UNLIKE THE PROCESSIONAL, which celebrates the bride, the recessional pays homage to the couple. The end of the wedding service is inevitably followed by a burst of euphoria that signals the couple's union and a joyous sense of completion. With music playing, attendants filing past, guests in rapt attention and the beaming bride and groom, the recessional celebrates all the glorious possibilities of commitment.

▪ As they walk down the aisle, the couple should take the time to acknowledge family and guests. In the excitement of the moment, most couples tend to race down the aisle, leaving guests little opportunity to revel in their joy. ▪ The recessional music should inspire a sense of gaiety and celebration. ▪ For interesting perspectives, the photographer and videographer should be stationed in front and in back of the newlyweds.

Three divine brides with extraordinary bouquets. *Above* Newlyweds Marisol and Rob Thomas take time for a wedding kiss as they proceed down the aisle at their outdoor ceremony, October 2, 1999, 7pm, Santa Ynez, California. *Opposite* Melissa Barrett Rhodes and James Rhodes take the opportunity to acknowledge family and friends as they leave the altar, October 5, 1996, 6:45pm, Brick Presbyterian Church, New York City. *Left* Robin and Chris Donahoe celebrate their wedding ceremony by stepping through a giant arbor of floral garlands in front of Saint Margaret's Episcopal Church, September 26, 1998, 7:30pm, Carrollton, Georgia.

THE CEREMONY DEPARTURE

The getaway

NOT TO BE CONFUSED with the recessional, the departure segment of the ceremony provides its own moment of wedding drama. Amid a flurry of flower petals, a hail of birdseed or scores of colorful butterflies, the newly married couple exits the ceremony to great fanfare and commotion. Needless to say, all of this so-called spontaneity must be carefully orchestrated.

SOME GUIDELINES ▪ Tossing material should be handed to the guests as they exit the venue. ▪ The photographer, videographer and any other participants, such as the driver, should be alerted in advance. ▪ While rice symbolizes fertility, it is also lethal for birds and certain wildlife, so choose an alternative for an outdoor ceremony. ▪ Balloons and fireworks are spectacular effects but are not always legal or environmentally correct, so be advised. ▪ If the entire wedding celebration is confined to one venue, such as a private home or a country club, this may preclude a dramatic ceremony exit for the bride and groom. A musical flourish or a shower of confetti may replace church bells, a waiting carriage and cheering guests.

Above Rachel and Franco DiCarlo descending the stone steps of the Basilica San Pietro with parents and attendants in tow, October 19, 1996, 11am, The Vatican, Rome, Italy. *Opposite* Carolina Zapf and John Josephson leaving their wedding service at The Church of Santa Maria, with three tiny attendants in a horse-drawn carriage, July 3, 1999, 5:30pm, Sintra, Portugal. *Right* Yvonne Force and Leo Villareal make a stylish ceremony departure from the Chapel of San Francisco in the Cathedral of Cuernavaca, November 14, 1998, 6pm, Cuernavaca, Mexico.

IN TERMS OF CAPTURING SENTIMENT, few things are as enduring as wedding photographs. So the choice of photographer and videographer will have lasting consequences.

SOME IDEAS TO KEEP IN MIND For a large wedding, two photographers can be better than one. If budget is not a concern, it may be a necessary extravagance to have one photographer for the conventional wedding portraits and another for the more interpretive shots. You may also prefer one photographer for the more artistic black and white photographs and another for the more spontaneous color shots.

MAKE A PRECISE LIST of each moment to be recorded and who should be included in the picture. If the photographers know what is expected of them in advance, chances are they will be infinitely more effective. PHOTOGRAPHERS should be conscious of the backgrounds and who and what appears in each frame. I am often disconcerted by the wedding pictures I see, as some appear cluttered, others poorly staged and some downright careless. While anything can be done with retouching, the costs are prohibitive. If a wedding venue is less than ideal, create a makeshift studio by using seamless paper as a backdrop. A clean background always looks elegant.

PHOTOGRAPHY AND FILM
Forever after

THE PHOTOGRAPHS SHOULD be scheduled so that everyone, particularly the bride, feels relaxed. I tried to anticipate most contingencies during my wedding, but if I had it to do over again, I would definitely have given more care to my formal wedding portraits. Start an hour earlier if it means getting all the desired pictures.

▪ Proper lighting is key to producing flattering pictures. ▪ A successful wedding video demands the expertise of a professional. ▪ Inform the photographer and videographer as to who will be working that day. Certain photographers have been known to refuse to work alongside anyone else. ▪ As many photographers retain ownership of the film, clarify this point before signing a contract. ▪ Providing each guest with a disposable camera can frequently result in some of the more fantastic and spontaneous shots. ▪ After the wedding, pictures and multiple copies of the video should be ordered immediately — our tape was erased and along with it any record of our special day. ALWAYS ANTICIPATE the unexpected. Provisions should be made for equipment failure, defective film, poor lighting, bad weather or illness. For photographs, it is impossible to be too prepared.

Above Melissa Barrett Rhodes and James Rhodes pose for their traditional wedding portrait during the cocktail hour before joining guests at their reception, October 5, 1996, 7:30pm, University Club, New York City. *Opposite* There is such a timeless quality to black and white photographs. A charming portrait of Oriko and Kunimasa Kume after their superb wedding ceremony, October 7, 1996, 2:30pm, Tokyo, Japan.

THE WEDDING ALBUM Photo albums are the most tangible documentation of the wedding day. The task of assembling them, however, is often postponed or altogether abandoned. Make time to organize your albums as soon as the pictures arrive.

BLACK AND WHITE VS. COLOR VS. DIGITAL FILM ▪ Black and white photos are generally more artistic than color, yet they are also far more costly, due to special processing and reprinting charges. ▪ Images recorded digitally are stored and printed through a computer. ▪ Color photographs also look festive and true to life; however, special attention should be given to backdrops and close-ups.

BECAUSE THE PROCESS of film development is so expensive, most pictures are presented in one of three formats: print, proof or contact sheet.

PRINTS These are photographs that have been enlarged from original negatives. There will be an extra charge for cropping, retouching or blowups.

PROOFS Always submitted in preliminary books or "proof boxes," proofs are shots that have been numbered and arranged to facilitate selection. Any variations, such as tinting, cropping or retouching, will incur additional cost.

CONTACT SHEETS A contact sheet is a miniature compilation of each photograph on a roll of film. Choices should be indicated with a grease pencil. Often, a photographer will submit the contact sheets slightly enlarged to make the selection process somewhat easier. Any special effects will increase the cost.

FOR BUDGETARY REASONS, edit judiciously. Couples who wed during high season should expect to wait four to six months for an album. As the design of a wedding album is completely subjective, it is best to seek professional advice.

▪ Normally, a wedding photographer reproduces pictures in standard 8x10 format. If a specific measurement is desired, however, he should be alerted. ▪ Each album should be bound in a durable material such as leather or fabric. It should also include acid-free paper, matting, double-bound archival paper and taped corners to secure each photograph. ▪ A monogram or a bookmark of silk ribbon adds a personal and subtle touch to a wedding album.

Opposite Renowned fashion photographer Arthur Elgort as a guest at our wedding. Arthur always brings his camera everywhere. Luckily for us, he created his own images of our celebration, which we still cherish today. Vera Wang and Arthur Becker, June 22, 1989, 9pm, The Pierre Hotel, New York City. *Opposite above* One of the most sophisticated wedding albums I have ever seen belongs to Elizabeth and Jeff Louis. From the handbound volumes, the archival paper and the acid-free tissue to the subtle monogramming and delicate silk ribbon binders, these albums are positively inspiring.

THE COCKTAIL HOUR

The high art of entertaining

WHILE THE WEDDING CEREMONY is entirely devoted to ritual and pageantry, the cocktail hour is intended for fun and acknowledging loved ones. Less formal and more relaxed than the religious portion of the wedding or the reception, the cocktail hour serves as a much-needed transition from the serious tenor of the ceremony to the joyous abandon of the celebration. EVEN IF IT IS SIMPLY a walk into an adjacent room, once the couple is off to the cocktail hour, their obligations as hosts begins.

■ For receptions in an obscure location or one that is far from the ceremonial venue, it may be necessary to provide transportation. ■ If rented vehicles such as buses or limousines are not feasible, designated drivers should guide guests to the reception. Otherwise, directions and a map should be included with each invitation. ■ Parking can also become a serious concern. For my brother Ken's wedding in Westchester County, guests had to park their cars at a golf course and be bussed to the reception. In New York City, for our wedding, the parking issue was compounded because many garages near our venue were full. ■ Mother nature, too, can turn an easy trip into a travel nightmare. Fog, snow, freezing cold and darkness can confound even the most accommodating guest. ■ If the cocktail hour takes place in an adjoining room, the decoration, music and food should create a total shift in ambiance. ■ In Europe, couples are required by law to get married at City Hall. As this is usually followed by a reception later that day, issues of transportation and logistics should be addressed first. ■ For weddings in a foreign country, the hosts may be obliged to supply transportation and lodging. ■ The most considerate touch a host can offer is an easy transition from the ceremony to the cocktail hour.

Opposite Even the color of a champagne cocktail can lend a festive and imaginative touch to the celebration. *Above* Crisp white cotton aprons are the perfect accessory for waiters at an outdoor wedding in a vineyard.

THE RECEIVING LINE AND MARRIAGE CONTRACTS Immediately following the ceremony, a traditional receiving line is usually formed by members of the bridal party for the express purpose of welcoming guests. The etiquette of standing in deliberate formation to greet each person is a heartfelt way of acknowledging their friendship and support.

TO AVOID A CONSPICUOUS BREAK in the festivities, the number of individuals in the receiving line should be limited to the bride and the groom, their respective parents and any children belonging to either party. The only exceptions may be a close, elderly relative or an important family member.

THE ORDER MIGHT BE ▪ The bride followed by the groom, the mother of the bride, the father of the bride, the mother of the groom, the father of the groom. ▪ The mother of the bride, the father of the bride, the bride, the groom, the mother of the groom, the father of the groom. ▪ The mother of the bride, the mother of the groom, the father of the bride, the father of the groom, the bride and the groom. ▪ The mother of the bride, the bride, the father of the bride, the mother of the groom, the groom and the father of the groom. ▪ Children should stand next to their parents.

AS MANY BRIDES PREFER NOT TO BE VIEWED prior to the ceremony, their formal portraits may be scheduled during the cocktail hour. Other couples are required by custom or religion to sign their marriage contracts upon completion of the ceremony. In both instances, the newlyweds must forgo the ritual of a receiving line for more immediate wedding obligations. If the ceremony is inordinately long or takes place outdoors, the bride and the groom may wish to take this opportunity to relax or regroup. For some Asian brides, this is the moment to change into their next gown. AS THE NEWLYWEDS are the primary focus of the celebration, if they anticipate skipping the cocktail hour, an alternative form of entertainment should be provided for the guests. Strolling violinists, an elaborate buffet or a mesmerizing sunset can all be enchanting metaphors for this transitional portion of the wedding.

BEVERAGES AND FOOD

THE MOST SEDUCTIVE COCKTAIL PARTIES have three important ingredients: incredible hors d'oeuvres, imaginative drinks and fantastic music. Whether it's Beluga caviar or pigs-in-a-blanket, cold martinis or ice-cold beer, the presentation of food and drink should be as inventive as it is appetizing. As I often prefer finger food to big meals, cocktails to vintage champagne and serenades to disco, the cocktail hour is one of my favorite parts of the wedding celebration.

■ Adequate chairs and tables should be supplied for guests. Nothing is more frustrating than trying to negotiate food, drink and conversation with nowhere to sit. ■ There must be adequate bartenders and servers, so guests need not wait in line. Passed champagne and wine are an added extravagance. ■ Even during daytime, tiny lamps or scented candles lend ambiance and an air of sophistication to the cocktail tables. ■ Freshly cut flowers always provide fragrance and enormous visual beauty. ■ For elaborate buffets, replete with sushi bars, caviar bowls, ice sculptures and trays of hors d'oeuvres, the cocktail hour might be scheduled before the ceremony, so guests have an opportunity to recover before dinner. FOR A LIMITED BUDGET, a great cocktail party can be a wonderful alternative to a formal dinner. A wedding celebration should always be a fun gathering of friends that falls within affordable limits. The most successful celebrations are those that respect financial boundaries.

Above left and below For Jodi Della Femina's ceremony on the beach, this candlelit stairwell served as both the wedding aisle and an imaginative passage to the cocktails. The lush buffets at her cocktail hour were laden with voluptuous flowers and leaves that cascaded over the tabletops onto the grass. Huge jars of exotic drinks were served with wooden ladles. *Top right* For Jamie and Steve Tisch's wedding celebration, the gardens were furnished with white linen, skirted cocktail tables and gold ballroom chairs with matching seat cushions. White votive candles wrapped in ribbon and colorful centerpieces accented with white roses provided an artistic touch.

THE ESCORT TABLE

During cocktails, the escort table serves as a necessary and functional guide to the seating at a formal wedding reception. A typical escort table provides a card with each guest's name, table number and seat. Whether it's a formal lunch or a dinner dance, the wrong seat assignment or failing to locate one's table can be incredibly frustrating. While last minute changes are inevitable, fewer adjustments mean fewer mistakes. THE LOCATION of the escort table is also critical. The table should be clearly designated and easily accessible. If the decoration is too extravagant, guests may overlook the table altogether. For a large wedding there should be at least one person there to direct. LIKE INVITATIONS and wedding programs, place cards, menus and escort cards should conform to the style of the celebration. They always help minimize confusion and alleviate anxiety for everyone. The size of the print should be clearly legible for all guests to read.

Above From the formality of classical musicians serenading guests in New York City to the calypso group Ban Caribe in Greenwood, Virginia, the range in musical styles is limitless. *Left* The Monterey String Quartet entertains guests at a wedding in Pebble Beach, California. *Right* A jazz quartet provides background atmosphere at a garden wedding in Sintra, Portugal.

WHILE A MARRIAGE CEREMONY EXUDES an aura of splendor and solemnity, the reception, like the cocktail hour, is entirely dedicated to celebrating the bride and groom. Unlike the wedding service, the design and décor for the reception need not conform to any preconceived notion of religious ritual. AS MOST WEDDING RECEPTIONS are predominantly focused on the meal, the food presentation and the design of the tables will clearly impact the overall décor. Whether it is a grosgrain ribbon tied around a napkin fold for a restaurant wedding or an entire field tented for an afternoon lunch, decoration is any detail that lends a special touch to the reception. FOR MOST COUPLES, the reception represents the greatest expense. Depending, however, on how they maximize spending, a reception can be imaginatively achieved on any budget.

THE RECEPTION

Celebrating the couple

IF TREMENDOUS EMPHASIS IS TO BE PLACED on the food and wine, candles can be just as effective a way of creating ambiance as flowers are. Should the reception be a stylish cocktail buffet, the most important decoration might be the centerpieces. Issues of budget and how it impacts the decoration should always be a primary wedding consideration.

SOMETIMES A HOLIDAY CELEBRATION offers a clever motif for the entire reception, whether it's a sprig of mistletoe placed over the doorway of a barn, yards of Christmas lights, tiny American flags, or Valentines tucked into the napkins. The most memorable weddings are always the most personal ones.

SOME GENERALITIES ▪ As the primary focus of the reception will be on the tables and the food presentation, anticipate how they will look before settling on a location. ▪ Certain extraordinary venues may be challenging or less costly to decorate. While a beautiful room with intricate detailing or a breathtaking view might initially appear very expensive, it could end up costing less in terms of decoration. ▪ Receptions that are exceptionally formal frequently necessitate more costly decorations. More, however, is not necessarily more elegant. ▪ Sometimes an intimate reception can be more opulent than a larger one. ▪ While imaginative, an off-site location such as a museum, concert hall, cruise ship or nightclub may entail additional costs, complex legal ramifications or security issues.

Creating the various tables for the wedding reception requires a penchant for detail, a love of entertaining and a true appreciation for food and drink. *Opposite* For the wedding celebration of Mr. and Mrs. William J. Diggins III, no expense was spared, from the silverware and linens to the extraordinary floral centerpieces. *Above* During an extremely lengthy cocktail hour, I changed into my next dress, as per Chinese wedding custom, and then redid my hair. Finally, Arthur and I were ready to rejoin our guests with a grand entrance for our first dance.

Sometimes, a low centerpiece offers a subtle counterpoint to other more extravagant floral schemes. From a giant urn filled with flowering branches to a mantel or chandelier draped in blossoms, flowers always provide the ultimate sense of luxury at a wedding reception.

THE RECEPTION LIGHTING

How we look and feel depends on it

FOR ALL SEGMENTS OF THE WEDDING, I cannot emphasize enough the relevance of lighting. The general atmosphere, as well as the guest's level of comfort and confidence, rely on it. Ideally, lighting should soften and enhance. The right lighting makes everyone feel more attractive, while harsh lighting compromises even the most beautiful bride. Where photography is concerned, bad lighting can magnify the slightest flaw. THE POSSIBILITIES FOR DECORATIVE LIGHTING are limitless. A roaring fire in the great room of a log cabin is every bit as seductive as a seaside terrace bathed in starlight and candles. Enormous candelabra with crystal bowls provide just as much dramatic emphasis as pinpoint lighting on a simple orchid plant. LIKE EVERY OTHER aspect of wedding decoration, lighting should be designed to highlight specific wedding rituals, such as the first dance, the wedding toasts, the cake cutting and the tossing of the bouquet.

Above Sharon Stone chose to center her enormous wedding table around the goldfish pool in the backyard of her home in Los Angeles. *Opposite* Producer Steve Tisch and his wife, Jamie, preferred to illuminate their wedding tables at both the rehearsal dinner and the reception with long graceful tapers. I found their choice of wedding venue to be especially charming and festive. October 8, 1996, 8pm, Merryvale Vineyard, Napa Valley, California.

This page above Even the youngest guests at Whitney and Lee Brown's wedding were given their own set of sparklers, June 3, 2000, 11pm, Onwentsia Club, Lake Forest, Illinois. *Below* Elizabeth and Jeff Louis and guests celebrate their wedding with a private display of fireworks at the Shedd Aquarium, June 26, 1996, 10pm, Chicago, Illinois. *Opposite* Fireworks light up the night sky at the wedding of Mr. and Mrs. Thomas F. Wessel in St. Jean Cap Ferrat, France.

▪ For those who have engaged a lighting engineer, there is no limit as to the special effects that can be achieved today, from laser shows to fireworks displays. As too much technology can sometimes be a bit overwhelming, use discretion. ▪ If the reception takes place in an unexceptional venue, excessive lighting may focus too much attention on the surroundings. In such cases, it is usually best to forgo an excess of special effects. ▪ Sometimes, effective lighting can actually camouflage poor architecture or help to redefine a space. Anticipate the lighting plan early on. ▪ Lighting a dance floor always requires special practical and decorative considerations. ▪ It is always important to make use of any available natural light. Sunlight provides its own sense of gaiety and charm, as well as a different kind of ambiance.

AS FOOD REPRESENTS the primary focal point of the reception, everything centers around the wedding tables and their visual appeal. Careful attention should be paid to each specific nuance, no matter how insignificant it may seem.

IT IS DIFFICULT to devise an effective seating plan until the floorplan of the room has been determined. COMBINING DIFFERENT SHAPES of tables in one room can be whimsical and appealing: rectangular, square, round, oval, V-shaped or U-shaped. Extreme proportions can also be intriguing and unexpected. Depending upon the scale of the room, an extra long table could be used for the bridal party, with spacious squares for the children and smaller rounds for the older guests. A giant U-shaped table around a reflecting pool or an enormous rectangle provide drama and an unusual sense of scale.

THE WEDDING TABLES
The tables define the reception

- Table linens for standard shapes are usually less expensive to rent than custom sizes. ▪ While a crowded table encourages conversation, more elbowroom is luxurious and facilitates dining. ▪ The stability of the table matters — nothing is as annoying as a wobbly surface. ▪ A thin underpad protects the tabletop and enhances the appearance of table linens. ▪ The bridal table should always stand out: an unusual shape or proportion, draped chairs or more extravagant decoration differentiates the newlyweds' table from that of their guests. ▪ For an unusually large reception, there should be some way to designate those who are seated farther away. Perhaps the tables could have a more important centerpiece or the same configuration as that of the wedding party. ▪ As everyone cannot be positioned near the bride and groom, seat those most inclined to dance near the dance floor.

Where reception venues are concerned, I am generally a stickler about the architectural details of a room, the dance floor in particular. Nothing lends more dignity to a wedding venue than an incredible floor. Even plain tables look more important on a beautiful surface. Both rooms featured here have extraordinary moldings, wood paneling and lighting fixtures, to say nothing of the floor and ceilings. They provide the perfect backdrop for staging a reception. *Above* October 3, 1998, 5:30pm, Sleepy Hollow Country Club, Scarborough, New York. *Right* The wedding of Mr. and Mrs. Darren R. Schuringa, April 12, 1997, 8:30pm, University Club, New York City. *Left* One of the most lavish wedding receptions I have ever attended was that of Christine and Richard Mack. As there were more than 500 guests, silver chargers and candelabra were an enormous luxury.

ON FLOWERS AND DECORATION ▪ While flowers represent an enormous expense, they also provide beauty, symbolism and fragrance. ▪ Any details, such as hand-rolled flowers on a wedding gown or the bride's bouquet, may reference some of the decorations for the reception. A delicate grosgrain ribbon or some sophisticated color, like pearl gray or champagne, can also add a delicate accent. ▪ To avoid total conformity, each centerpiece could be fashioned out of different varieties of flowers. ▪ Dark tablecloths look sumptuous with pale or brightly colored flowers for an evening wedding. ▪ If the decoration budget is limited, greenery such as English ivy, garlands or even boxes of grass can be charming substitutes for flowers. So can rented trees, carved topiaries or English privet for an indoor reception. ▪ Chaffs of wheat or symbolic herbs combined with colorful fruits and seasonal vegetables look painterly and imaginative for a less formal reception. ▪ Strategically placed urns filled with extravagant flowers provide emphasis and eliminate the need for centerpieces on every table. ▪ For an exceptional venue, any architectural or decorative element in a room can be highlighted, whether it is a wall sconce, a fireplace mantel or a period chandelier. ▪ For a less formal buffet or a backyard celebration, a single rose on each plate could double as a party favor and a decoration. ▪ Presentation is everything, and nowhere does that become more apparent than at a reception.

THE CHAIRS Chairs are another important design consideration, especially if there are one hundred of them in a room. As there are surprisingly few rental styles to choose from, some attempt should be made to personalize them. Seat covers or cushions can help. So can greenery. No matter what the decorative decisions, comfort should be a central concern as well. Chairs for the reception must not only be attractive, but be sturdy and, above all, maneuverable. Whether the chairs are fold-up, ballroom, painted or slipcovered, they make as big a statement as the tables themselves. As the guests will invariably spend more time at their tables than the bride and groom will at theirs, keep their comfort level in mind.

TABLETOPS Depending upon the style, the tabletop decoration can go from starkly minimal to seriously baroque. Again, design and budget are key considerations. The process of decorating the tables can begin anywhere – a special plate, a favorite flower or a beautiful piece of fabric can all serve as inspiration.

THE CHINA Most commercial wedding venues supply their own china, as do hotels and caterers. If generic plates have little appeal and budget permits, it is possible to rent dinnerware from party rental facilities. Pure white china is a flawless way of presenting food, while decorated patterns can look quite dramatic. Keep the plates in mind when choosing the flatware. Metal trims and finishes may become significant issues when coordinating silverware with stemware and china.
■ A simple white plate best highlights a sophisticated food presentation. ■ White china always appears wonderfully dramatic on a dark tablecloth. ■ Any decorative detail like a rose, a ribbon or scattered flower petals can transform a simple plate. ■ Unmatched china can look stylish and inventive, as long as the pairing is deliberately inconsistent and one hundred guests are not being served. ■ When choosing one's table linens, do not overlook china, stemware and flatware. ■ Less formal china is always appropriate for an outdoor wedding. ■ Buffet plates should always be oversized. ■ Plates look more elegant with less food on them.

NAPKINS From a simple roll to a Bishop's hat, a carefully articulated napkin fold is an effective and artistic way to bring design interest to a wedding table. To personalize each place setting, an interesting napkin-fold can also add design emphasis to a plain piece of china. Although solid white napkins highlight more elaborate folds, a decorative fabric such as silk damask or shantung can provide contrast, texture and color. Where a napkin is positioned is another decorative style consideration.

For a less formal reception, any variation on a classical place setting can offer a refreshing alternative. *Above* The simplicity of basic elements focuses greater attention on each individual piece, from the delicacy of a gingham ribbon to the subtlety of a plain napkin fold. *Opposite* Linear rows of terra-cotta potted ferns create a powerful geometry, while pure-white china further defines the long rectangular tables.

THE SILVERWARE Inappropriate silverware is always a frustrating experience for any guest. Sometimes a generic place setting may not be enough. For example, with steaks or prime rib, steak knives are a must. If Chinese or Asian food is being served, chopsticks and traditional Western utensils are both necessary. When serving espresso, do not forget to provide demitasse spoons.

REGARDLESS of the formality of the menu, providing the proper flatware is essential. Select flatware to complement the table linens, the centerpiece and all the other decorations.

THE STEMWARE Traditional table settings require a glass for red wine, a glass for white wine and a water glass. For a formal wedding reception or seated dinner, the champagne glass is set at the table for a first course or provided later by the staff for the toasts.

IF THE CELEBRATION IS DECIDEDLY informal or ethnic in nature, replace both wineglasses with one all-purpose glass. Special drinking vessels such as sake cups or beer steins add an imaginative touch.

I ADORE SHADES of tinted crystal: green, red, blue, amethyst or amber. Colors can be dramatic in any combination. If gold-edged or etched stemware is preferred, every other element of the table should be coordinated with it. To avoid accidents or breakage, glasses should be stable and well-balanced.

PLACE CARDS A place card denotes the location of a guest's seat. If flowers are too costly, a place card can become a design element when combined with an interesting napkin fold or elegant candles. Whether they are handwritten or handmade, the place card is as necessary for a seated buffet as it is for a sit-down dinner.

THE MENU CARDS Although this formality is normally reserved for sit-down receptions, a menu card is a wonderful keepsake for any scale of reception. It usually highlights the date of the wedding, as well as the names or initials of the bride and groom. For formal celebrations, menu cards can double as place cards with each guest's name hand-lettered on top. It is also perfectly correct to assign one menu card to every couple. The style and details of the menu card should reinforce the decorative scheme of the table.

THE FAVORS Party favors should be positioned on the wedding tables next to each place setting. They should also be clearly visible in case a guest has to depart early. A piece of the groom's cake, a small box of fine chocolates or a pair of lacquered chopsticks can be a commemorative and thoughtful way to say thank-you.

Left Tiny gold boxes of Godiva chocolates lend warmth to the crispness of an all-white decorative scheme. Pearl-handled silverware offers a sophisticated accent for a daytime wedding table. *Opposite* The understated elegance of white linen napkins deliberately folded in a classic rectangular shape is meant to enhance the simple refinement of these outdoor wedding table settings.

ON FOOD AND DRINK Everything depends on the budget. That said, it is important that the bridal couple devote serious attention to their menu. What courses, which wines and the selection of desserts and after-dinner liqueurs all require thorough consideration. Like flowers, alcohol can represent a gigantic expense. Most beverage professionals, however, can achieve clever solutions even if finances preclude vintage champagnes or rare wines.

- Special diets, such as vegetarian, kosher, religion-based and health-restricted, should be accommodated. Allergies to shellfish, dairy, nuts or certain fruits, like strawberries or papaya, should be noted. ▪ Courses should be easy to handle. Light is always best at a wedding. ▪ Avoid heavily seasoned dishes. ▪ Courses should be kept to a minimum, unless the reception is held in a four-star restaurant. ▪ Some dishes are difficult to prepare for large numbers of guests. Factor this into the menu selection. ▪ Service must be timely. ▪ Beverages such as freshly squeezed juices, nonalcoholic ciders or lightly flavored sodas should be available for nondrinkers. ▪ Diet sodas should be provided for those with specific health concerns. ▪ If the reception is in a hotel, a catering hall or a restaurant, negotiate the beverage contract up front. Where possible, supply the liquor yourself, for a great savings.

CATERING If a party planner is not in the budget, a full-service caterer can resolve many concerns, from the menu, the service and the rental equipment to the bars, coat checks, parking and other logistics.

THE FIRST STEP is the menu. The caterer should collaborate on an inventive menu that reflects the preferences of the bridal couple. Regardless of the menu choice, one food-tasting is a prerequisite.

SMALLER CATERING COMPANIES may supply only the food, leaving equipment rentals up to the client. Since most rental companies are adept at dealing with weddings, resolving this could be as simple as a telephone call. Sometimes a caterer can also be a party planner. Besides providing food and services, he can subcontract and supervise the location, florist, musicians, lighting and other wedding details. If the reception is in a hotel or a private club, the resident banquet manager assumes the duties of a caterer.

FINAL CONSIDERATIONS ▪ Ample room should be made for guests and waiters to circulate freely. ▪ Beware of fire hazards. ▪ Temperature and ventilation play a significant role in everyone's comfort level. ▪ If the ceremony and reception are in the same venue, anticipate how long it will take to "turn" the room. ▪ For large weddings, ample lavatories should be a consideration.

THE DANCE FLOOR AND THE STAGE

For dancing, circulating, people watching or "perching," the dance floor assumes important design and decorative significance. The positioning of the dance floor in relation to the guests and the orchestra can also influence the overall outcome of the reception. Frequently, too little attention is paid to the stage. After all the other expenses, the wrong set up can diminish the elegance of the entire reception.

■ The dance surface must be secured, particularly if it is suspended over a pool or tennis court. ■ Wind is a key consideration out-of-doors. Any decoration, whether it is a special chandelier, a giant arbor, dripping moss or paper lanterns, should be safely secured. ■ There must be safe and easy access for everyone. Walking down a dark garden path does not qualify as safe. ■ There should be ample space for guests to dance. ■ The only thing worse than an empty dance floor is an overcrowded one. Approximately eight square feet per couple is a good rule of thumb. ■ Because it is so highly visible, a painted dance floor or special decorative floor pattern can add significant design interest to the reception. ■ The stage or backdrop should always be coordinated with the other decorations. Where possible, a removable podium should be anticipated for speeches and toasts. ■ The performers' attire should coincide with the backdrop and tenor of the wedding. ■ Insurance should be secured, in case of mishaps.

ON MUSIC

If there is to be dancing at the reception, nothing effects the pace or the pleasure of a celebration more than music. Issues of sound, stage, lighting and dance floor, however, can present tremendous design challenges, space considerations and untold costs. Although it may be difficult to envision a wedding reception without music, even with limited finances, there are many imaginative solutions.

■ Audition any special groups or soloists. ■ All music should be selected carefully and with equal consideration for guests of all ages. ■ The music provider should anticipate such wedding traditions as the first dance or the horah, a given for Jewish ceremonies. A musical flurry that accompanies an announcement may be necessary to get everyone's attention, particularly at a large wedding. ■ If a full-piece orchestra has already been engaged for the reception, a disc jockey or additional entertainment might be necessary during band breaks. Ideally, this should not conflict with the general mood of the celebration. ■ Audio speakers should be kept at a safe distance, especially for those seated nearest to the orchestra or sound system. ■ Even a solo violinist can create magic. ■ A dedicated music provider, willing partners, adequate space and good ventilation are all needed to provide the proper environment for dancing. Guests should be seated together so everyone has an opportunity to enjoy a dance.

WHERE ROMANCE IS CONCERNED, the most enchanting moment of the wedding is the first dance. All eyes are focused on the bride and groom and for that instant, anything is possible. There is something so incredibly captivating about a couple expressing their love publically for one another. A GRACEFUL WALTZ or a sensual tango, the style is less significant than the sentiment of the couple's first dance together as man and wife. This peculiar blend of intimacy and exhibitionism makes the first dance one of the most intriguing images of the wedding.

A FEW PRACTICAL SUGGESTIONS ▪ The bride's train should be securely bustled and her veil rechecked, if she intends to wear it. ▪ While there are no precise rules, the first dance could be scheduled for when the couple first enters the reception, in order to maximize drama. ▪ Shoes should be scored with a pair of scissors to avoid slipping. ▪ Parents or guardians from both families should be advised of the timing, so they can participate. ▪ The music provider or emcee, along with the photographer and videographer, should be alerted well in advance. ▪ The choice of music should have special meaning for the couple. ▪ The first dance should never go on interminably.

THE FIRST DANCE
True romance

Left Sharon Stone and Phil Bronstein, Valentine's Day, 1998, evening, Los Angeles, California. *Opposite* Annette Roque Lauer and Matt Lauer, October 3, 1998, 7pm, a private residence, Water Mill, New York.

Above The first dance of Melissa Rivers and John Endicott at their Russian-inspired wedding, December 12, 1998, 10pm, Grand Ballroom, The Plaza Hotel, New York City. *Opposite* Carlin Gillin takes a whirl around the dance floor with a close friend at her wedding reception, June 10, 2000, 6pm, The Fairmont Copley Plaza, Boston, Massachusetts.

THE TOASTS

The gift of words

IF ONE'S FAMILY AND CIRCLE OF FRIENDS are as warm, enthusiastic and supportive as ours were, many guests may be motivated to make toasts. Due to the quantity of people involved, four hundred to be precise, we decided to limit the number of toasts and speeches at our wedding to just two. We also enjoyed the added surprise of a special serenade from my longtime friend, composer Martin Charnin. While my father's toast was moving and my father-in-law's heartfelt, the most memorable moment of the reception was Martin's impromptu rendition of his anthem, "Tomorrow," with lyrics written especially for us. We will always treasure this special gift of friendship.

- If the wedding is large, anticipate who might wish to speak and when.
- If the reception is intimate or informal, with no special entertainment to speak of, the toasts can provide a welcome diversion.
- If the bride and groom both wish to address the reception, their speeches should be relevant to all concerned.
- While a long speech can be moving, it can also be tedious, so keep it short and simple.
- Guests should be able to be videotaped at any time during the reception, so those who wish to participate may do so without having to stand up and make a public acknowledgment.
- Each guest should have a glass readily available for the toasts.
- Record all toasts and roasts on film.
- If needed, a musical flourish gets everyone's attention and adds a celebratory touch to the proceedings.
- The most heartfelt toasts and speeches are always spoken, not read.
- Allow extra time at the rehearsal dinner for additional speeches, toasts and roasts.

THE WEDDING CAKE

Decoration, symbolism, ritual, dessert

IF WEDDINGS ATTEST to our belief in commitment, then wedding cakes celebrate all that is fun and frivolous at the reception. A wedding cake is universally acknowledged as an object of extreme reverence and joy. THE MOST MEMORABLE CAKES are as imaginative as they are delicious. I personally love a bit of contrast or some element of surprise, such as morsels of fresh fruit inside layers of frosting or a chocolate cake under a sea of white butter cream. Texture is also important. SINCE MANY WEDDING VENUES have bakers on staff, they may require that the cake be made in-house, so the food contract should be checked. Study magazines, books and tear sheets for inspiration. If local bakers are uninspiring, it is feasible to have a cake shipped from another location. Most competent professionals have extensive look-books to peruse. CUTTING THE CAKE REPRESENTS THE START of the newlywed's life together. The groom places his right hand over the bride's to guide it for the first cut. Superstition requires that the bride cut the first piece. The groom feeds the bride, then she in turn feeds him. This shared piece of cake symbolizes their first meal together.

AS FORMAL TOASTS USUALLY FOLLOW the cutting of the cake, it is best to schedule this fairly early on. This is also an ideal opportunity for guests who wish to depart early to do so.

Top left A whimsical sand castle cake, complete with turret, for a beach wedding. The "sand" is actually flavored graham crackers over a mixed-berry shortcake. Jodi Della Femina and John Kim, July 8, 2000, 7pm, East Hampton, New York. *Top right* For Yvonne Force Villareal's wedding, the obvious theme of her cake was a sensuous tango. She definitely took the concept of the bride and groom on top of the cake to a whole new level. In all instances, I adore the look of wedding cakes seen at night. *Right* Here I am feeding Arthur a plate full of my favorite cake, *gateau aux pistaches*, at our reception, June 22, 1989, 11pm, Grand Ballroom, The Pierre Hotel, New York City.

Below Tennis great Mary Joe Fernandez prepares to cut her wedding cake with a little help from her husband, Tony Godsick, April 8, 2000, 10pm, Indian Creek Country Club, Miami, Florida. *Below left* Philippa Feigen Malkin chose a wedding confection adorned with colorful edible insects in honor of her husband's avocation, entomology. Cake by Le Nôtre, Paris, France.

THE GROOM'S CAKE

As he likes it

HISTORICALLY, the groom's cake is a dark, rich cake heavily laden with dried fruits, nuts and honey. Today, however, it can come in any shape, size, flavor or motif. It may be served as part of the dessert buffet, alongside the wedding cake, or sliced, wrapped in tissue and boxed with ribbon as a party favor. The groom's cake also provides an opportunity for the bride to highlight some of the groom's most endearing idiosyncrasies. As with the wedding cake, make certain that it tastes as good as it looks.

Left Unlike the elegant confections featured here, my husband's cake made joking reference to his obsession with golf, his love of tennis and his vegetable garden. *Above* Steve Tisch's cake was enough to inspire an evening gown in my collection. The marzipan grapes, leaves and vines not only reflected their choice of wedding venue, but the earthy colors of a vineyard.

THE BRIDE'S BOUQUET

To have, to hold and to toss

THERE IS ENORMOUS HISTORIC and emotional significance attached to a wedding bouquet. In ancient times, brides carried chaffs of wheat to invoke fertility and celebrate the joy of marriage. While brides today no longer adhere to this tradition, floral bouquets still embody the beauty and symbolism of this wedding ritual.

SOME THOUGHTS TO BEAR IN MIND
▪ Any decision regarding the gown or the decoration should be immediately shared with the florist or party designer. ▪ Left to the last minute, a bouquet can be a serious disaster with little or no relevance to the bride's gown or those of her bridal party. ▪ If an extravagant wedding gown is not a financial consideration, an extraordinary bouquet can serve to enhance a plain dress. ▪ If a dress is elaborate, the bouquet should be simple. ▪ As the bride's choice of flowers may not be seasonal, and thus expensive or impossible to procure, alert the florist as soon possible.

Above Melissa Barrett Rhodes giving an elegant toss of the bouquet to her attendants. *Center* Hands tell the tale. Philippa Feigen Malkin with a luscious bouquet of anemones in one hand and her husband's hand in the other. *Left* Connor McNally carrying my bouquet during the wedding processional.

While vibrant colors are great, I also love the subtlety of tonal bouquets. *Above* Lisa Hamlin with a divine bouquet of gardenias in the garden of her home after the wedding ceremony. *Opposite* My friend Elena Fiveyskovo-Lollos clutching an extravagant bouquet of cymbidium orchids and tiny pink hydrangea carefully designed to match her wedding gown.

■ A bad bouquet will undermine the most tasteful gown, while excess ribbons, ties and doilies can diminish even the most extraordinary flowers. ■ A bit of the bride's dress fabric can be used to decorate the bouquet. ■ If the bride's hands are otherwise occupied, as in a Jewish wedding ceremony, one of the young attendants can carry her bouquet. ■ If other accessories such as a hand muff or a bible are to be carried, the bouquet should be small and simple. ■ An enormous bouquet always looks disproportionate on a small bride. ■ For many day-time weddings, a fancy bouquet could detract from the elegance of the bride's attire. ■ For varied texture and proportion, certain species of small buds, such as freesia, lilies of the valley or baby's breath, can provide a delicate alternative to a nosegay. ■ A bouquet of some unexpected color, such as deep orange, black-red or purple, personalizes a traditional white wedding gown. ■ For more daring brides, an unusual lipcolor could be coordinated with that of the bouquet. ■ The bouquet could also be matched to the headpiece and corresponding details on the gown, a concept favored by English brides. ■ Bouquets look strange when the stems are completely enclosed, so the tips should always be visible. ■ All stems should be tapered so that the bride is not holding the equivalent of a tree trunk. ■ A heavy green leaf sometimes serves as a practical and decorative support for the rest of the bouquet. ■ Wait until the last possible minute to cut fresh flowers for the gown, headpiece or bouquet. ■ Dry towels should be made readily available since fresh bouquets are usually kept sitting in water. ■ If real flowers are to be worn in the hair or pinned to the back of the train, beware of pistils or petals that stain. ■ Allergies should always be a consideration. ■ If the bride intends to toss the bouquet, a second one should be made for just that purpose.

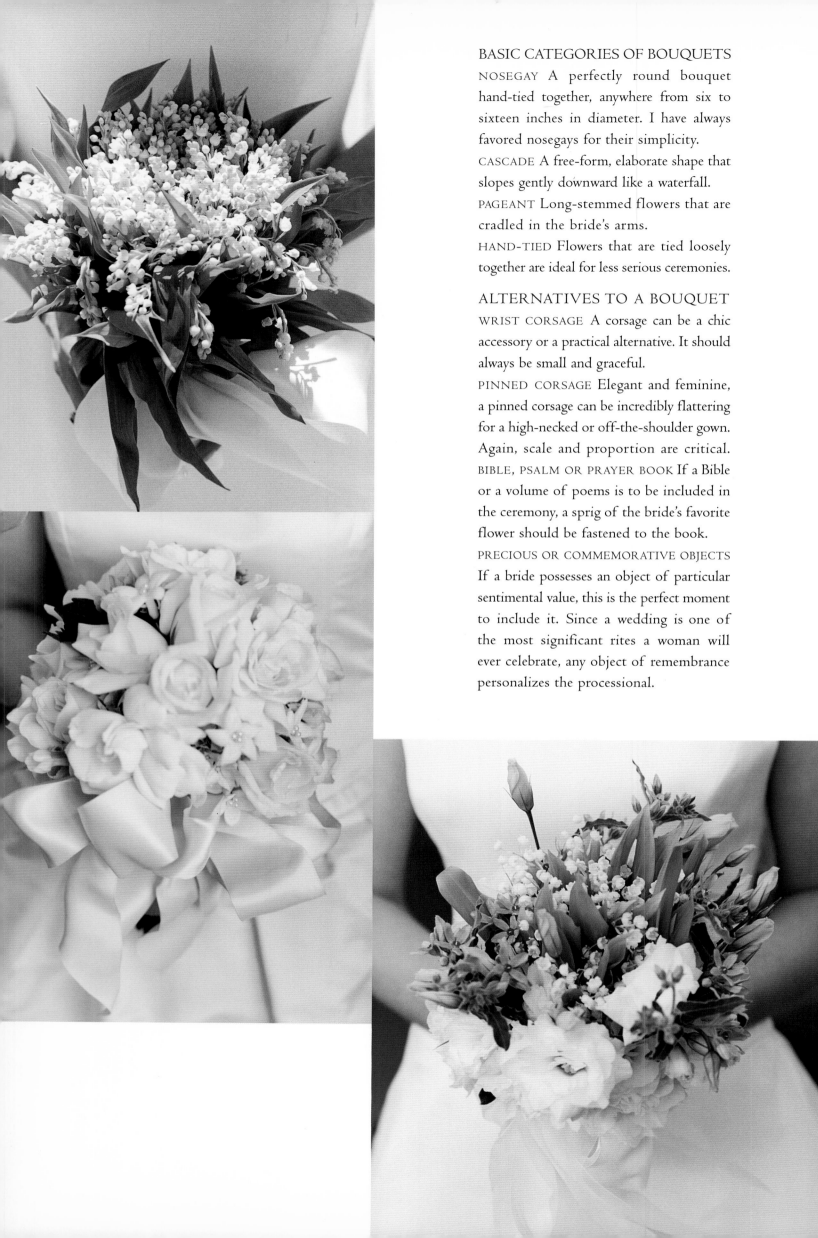

BASIC CATEGORIES OF BOUQUETS

NOSEGAY A perfectly round bouquet hand-tied together, anywhere from six to sixteen inches in diameter. I have always favored nosegays for their simplicity.

CASCADE A free-form, elaborate shape that slopes gently downward like a waterfall.

PAGEANT Long-stemmed flowers that are cradled in the bride's arms.

HAND-TIED Flowers that are tied loosely together are ideal for less serious ceremonies.

ALTERNATIVES TO A BOUQUET

WRIST CORSAGE A corsage can be a chic accessory or a practical alternative. It should always be small and graceful.

PINNED CORSAGE Elegant and feminine, a pinned corsage can be incredibly flattering for a high-necked or off-the-shoulder gown. Again, scale and proportion are critical.

BIBLE, PSALM OR PRAYER BOOK If a Bible or a volume of poems is to be included in the ceremony, a sprig of the bride's favorite flower should be fastened to the book.

PRECIOUS OR COMMEMORATIVE OBJECTS If a bride possesses an object of particular sentimental value, this is the perfect moment to include it. Since a wedding is one of the most significant rites a woman will ever celebrate, any object of remembrance personalizes the processional.

ONCE DEEMED A NECESSARY and symbolic part
of a woman's wardrobe, the garter survives today as
yet another beloved memento of the wedding ritual.
Traditionally, the groom removes the garter from
the bride's leg and tosses it to all of the remaining
bachelors. Supposedly, he who is lucky enough to
catch the garter is the next to become engaged.

THE WEDDING GARTER

The groom's to remove and to toss

■ Most garters are so overwrought
they are literally unwearable. For many
of my clients, I design special garters
to complement their gowns. ■ When
possible, choose a simple garter. It
should be unobtrusive enough to
be worn under even a narrow, bias
gown. ■ Two should be available – one
for tossing and one to keep. ■ A
blue wedding garter is the perfect
accessory for a superstitious bride.
■ As with other wedding traditions,
always alert the photographer as well
as the videographer. ■ Advise every
available bachelor of the garter toss.

Arthur tossing my pink silk garter to a group of
reluctant participants, June 23, 1989, 12:10am.

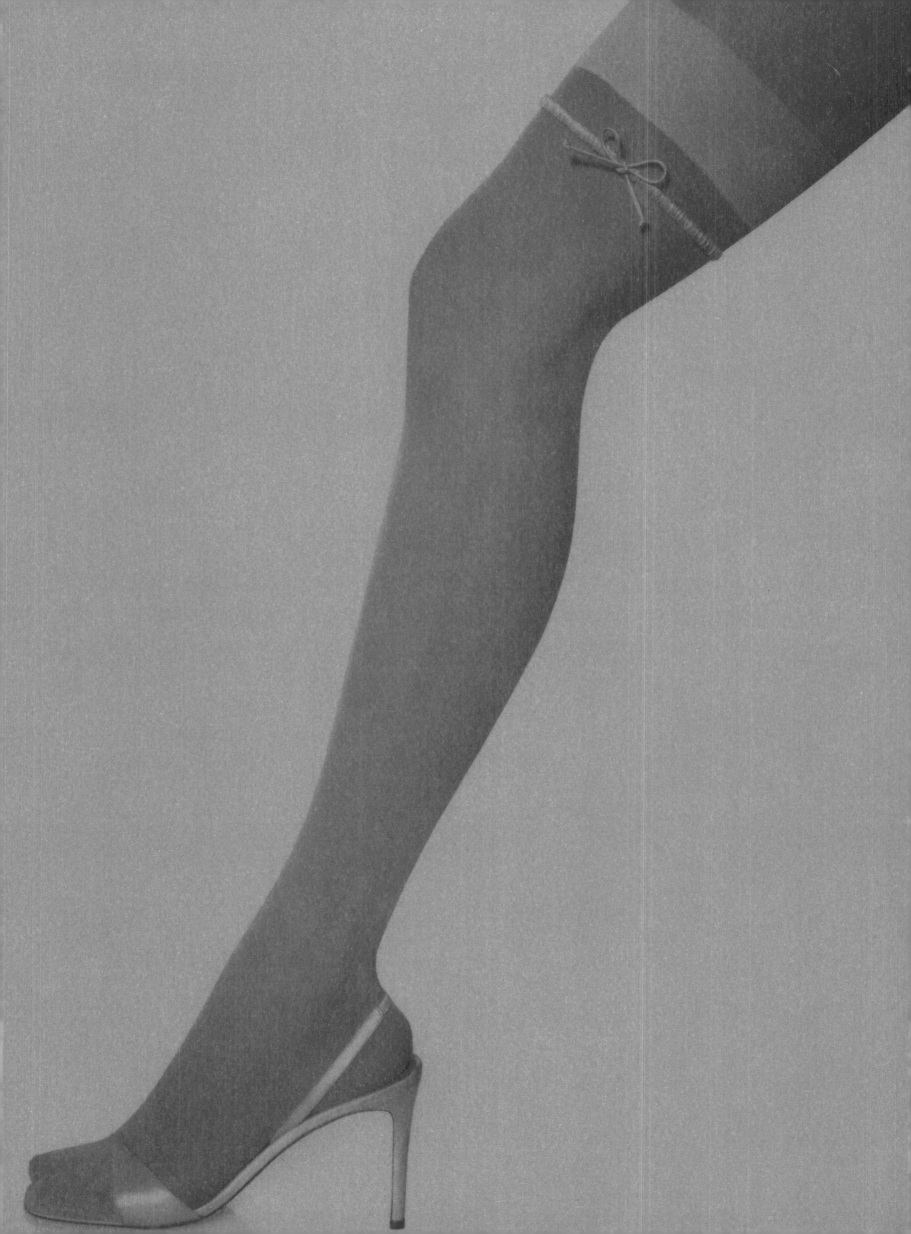

THE FINAL DEPARTURE

The great escape

AS SO MANY weddings today take place at night, there is frequently no big send-off for the bride and groom. Even more to the point, many couples are loath to leave their own receptions, preferring to while the night away with their closest pals and a cigar and cognac or another *coupe de champagne.* In our case, we actually watched our wedding decorations being dismantled in anticipation of the next wedding. ▪ In scripting the wedding scenario, the master of ceremonies or best man should advise all guests of the couple's intentions so everyone can be present for the departure. ▪ Decorate the car, carriage, bicycles or whatever for the final exit. ▪ If need be, have a change of attire handy. ▪ A midnight breakfast is a wonderful idea if the wedding celebration extends late into the night. ▪ A nightcap is the perfect opportunity to catch up with old friends or those who have made a great effort to be there.

Top A pair of exuberant newlyweds in a mad rush to leave the reception. The color of the convertible could not be more appropriate for a wedding. *Above* Guests glance skyward as the newlyweds make their final exit in a fantastical hot-air balloon. *Opposite* I find this vintage Rolls to be extraordinarily stylish – from the hand painted sign to the extravagant nosegay festooned with ribbons. Paula and Kenneth Brandes, October 3, 1998, 5pm, Belvedere Country Inn, Rhinebeck, New York.

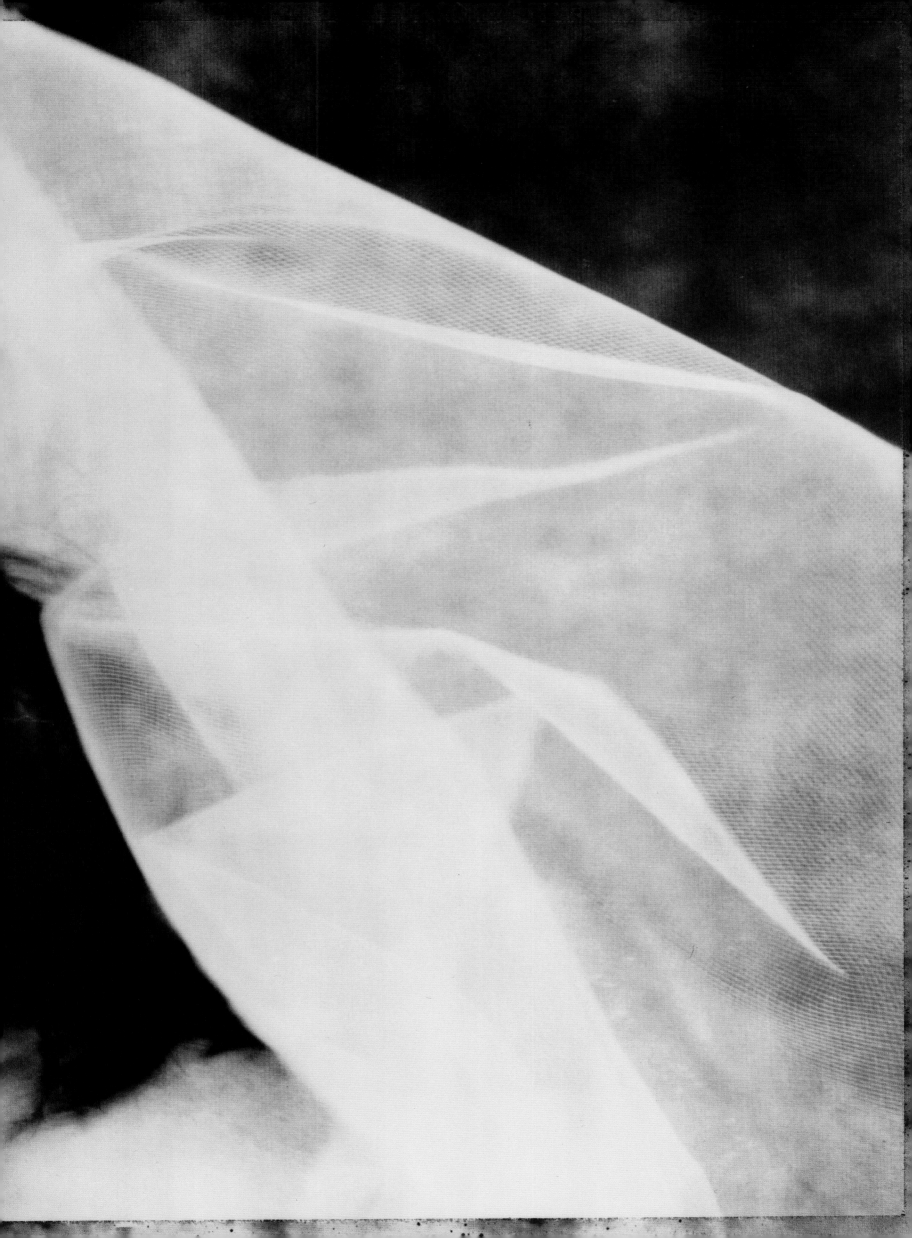

THE DIVINE OBSESSION

VERA WANG COUTURE COLLECTION
PHOTOGRAPHED BY PAOLO ROVERSI

FOR MOST WOMEN A WEDDING GOWN REPRESENTS FAR MORE THAN JUST A DRESS. IT IS ALSO THE EMBODIMENT OF A DREAM, PERHAPS ONE SHE HAS NURTURED SINCE CHILDHOOD. IN THIS FANTASY OF IDEALIZED HAPPINESS, THE GROOM REPRESENTS PERFECTION AND THE FACE OF ALL HUMAN POSSIBILITY. THE INSTANT A WOMAN BECOMES ENGAGED, HOWEVER, ALL THAT ENERGY AND PASSION GETS TRANSFERRED TO HER DRESS. WHAT FOLLOWS CAN BE SOMETHING AKIN TO MADNESS.

IMAGINE ALL THE COMPLEXITY OF HUMAN EMOTION AND EXPECTATION AT THE CROSSROADS OF FANTASY AND REALITY. THEN ADD CONSIDERATIONS OF TRADITION, PROPRIETY, SENSUALITY AND FASHION, AND CAPTURE ALL OF THAT IN ONE DRESS. IT ISN'T EASY.

WHILE A WOMAN HAS FEELINGS OF SELF-PERCEPTION FOR EVERY FACET OF LOVE, TODAY SHE HAS INFINITELY MORE POSSIBILITIES THAN EVER BEFORE. RULES ARE VANISHING. BARENESS IS NO LONGER TABOO, AND VEILS ARE NOT ALWAYS NECESSARY. FREEDOM AND INVENTION ABOUND.

WHETHER SHE IS SCHOOLMARM OR SIREN, FLOWER CHILD OR PRINCESS, SOCIALITE OR CAREER GIRL, OR A BIT OF EACH ROLLED INTO ONE, THE BRIDE SHOULD CHOOSE A GOWN THAT REFLECTS WHO SHE IS ABOVE AND BEFORE ALL ELSE. A WEDDING GOWN MUST ALWAYS EMBODY THE INDIVIDUAL.

A ONE-SHOULDER, CASHMERE-ALPACA, CARTRIDGE-PLEATED, FULL-SKIRTED WEDDING GOWN WITH CASCADING KIDSKIN FLOWERS. *Left*

THE TRADITIONALIST

A love of style always precedes fashion

The Traditionalist looks beyond fashion to style. This may involve careful assessment of all her features, strengths and flaws and how she can make them work to her best advantage. Everything she wears conveys a distinct message of confidence and an unyielding devotion to style. Style icons like Grace Kelly, Audrey Hepburn and Jacqueline Kennedy characterized a timeless beauty, poise and nonchalance that is still being emulated today. What they wore and how they looked seemed to express an effortless elegance. In reality, they were only being true to themselves – unique women with their own take on American style. The Traditionalist's allure stems from a subliminal kind of sex appeal. A natural inclination toward casual grace is part of her fascination. She is also a woman who intrigues others by inspiring an aura of curiosity. Her wedding gown is dignified and refined. Subtlety can be captivating, when what lingers in the mind is barely perceptible at first glance. For the Traditionalist, decoration should be distinctive yet understated, as with hand-tied bows, fabric-covered buttons, delicate lace trims or subtle embroidery. A Traditionalist's gown is always relevant and timeless.

A high-necked, long sleeved, ivory Alençon lace bodice over a full, satin-faced organza skirt with an opulent cathedral train and handmade buttons and loops.

THE MODERNIST

Through the eyes of a Modernist, the future is now

For a Modernist a sense of daring is always implied. Her frame of reference definitely represents an acquired taste, and one that arises from visualizing shapes in ever-changing contexts. Often rigorous or highly exaggerated, it also indicates a style of dress that requires thought. A Modernist design defies convention and frequently provides some rather extreme counterpoints. The wedding pouf I designed contrasts the stiffness of Duchess satin with the fragility of silk tulle. Plus, the collar functions as a hooded veil that rises from the shoulder. Sophisticated, no doubt, it also suggests the unusual blending of transparency and shape. For many, a Modernist's dress might appear to be more of a concept than something to wear. And, like art, it may not necessarily relate to daily life. It demands great intellect and energy to be a Modernist. A Modernist always looks forward. She is the ultimate nonconformist.

A bias Duchess satin pouf with funnel neck and flared sleeves.

THE SENSUALIST

A Sensualist finds pleasure in everything she wears

The Sensualist is obsessed with experiencing pleasure on every level. For her, a wedding gown should suggest, seduce and adorn. Fit is only secondary to comfort and ease, while texture and weight determine the outcome. The fabric should drape and fall suggestively against her skin with nothing to confine, restrict or bind. Luxury and extravagance equal sensuality. For this bride, a gossamer silk tulle veil or an ivory pashmina could be the ultimate wedding accessory. The Sensualist doesn't wear a dress, she experiences it. She delights in her body and revels in her powers of seduction. Physical sensitivity guides her every consideration, and style is a natural extension of her being. She regards clothing as part of her life, and her wedding gown as the ultimate tribute to her lifestyle. She is the quintessential courtesan.

A dress of thin kidskin with hand-embroidered eyelet by Vermont, Paris, for Vera Wang Couture.

THE INDIVIDUALIST

Her desire for self-expression transcends all other considerations

The Individualist will go to any length to make a deliberate fashion statement. Personal expression is key. Unlike the vast majority of brides, who embrace the convention of a white wedding gown, the Individualist prefers to follow her own dictates, whether that translates into the choice of an unusual color or a more unexpected silhouette. Her outward appearance reflects her innermost vision and every creative impulse. Headstrong and opinionated, she wears her individuality like a badge of honor. For the Individualist, her wedding attire provides the ultimate forum for self-expression. Although she may not set trends, she is most definitely not a follower. You can always rely on the Individualist to provide a hint of the unexpected.

A hand-embroidered empire silk taffeta-quilted dressing gown with split-panel sleeves and chapel train, worn over a bias silk chiffon slip.

THE ROMANTICIST

Passion guides her every decision

The Romanticist is ruled by higher passions than the reality of the world around her. She considers life a marvelous adventure and revels in the opportunity to realize her deepest emotions. The Romanticist is transported by a dress. For her, fantasy is always a reality. Her innate femininity and love of beauty can inspire a gown of great fragility and enchantment. Delicate ruffles, billowing sleeves or a lavish train fully bustled are some of the extravagant details that epitomize a romantic wedding gown. Whether it's a tulle confection worthy of Degas or an ode to Scarlett O'Hara, the Romanticist refuses to shy away from anything pretty. Her choice of attire never betrays her true nature. For her, looking girlish need not mean sacrificing style. Femininity and flirtation are her preferred tools of seduction, and she embraces them equally.

An ivory strapless satin-faced organza wedding gown with a skirt of hand-appliquéd concentric pinwheels of silk tulle. All appliqué work by Lemarié, Paris, France, for Vera Wang Couture.

For those who favor a spare aesthetic, a minimal wedding gown can be utter perfection. A Minimalist adores any version of clean, straightforward design with little or no excess. While

THE MINIMALIST

Less is always more

her clothes may often appear deceivingly simple, they are frequently anything but. True Minimalism requires a certain complexity of design and detail. It takes a confident individual to look minimal at her own celebration. Because a woman feels her most effusive just before a wedding, the bride who chooses a pared-down affect must maintain the discipline to edit when it can be so easy to add. For the right woman, a subtle wedding gown can make a powerful fashion statement. The unique appeal of a Minimalist lies in her purity of vision and the discipline to follow her convictions.

One-sleeved bias silk jersey ruched column wedding gown.

THE EXHIBITIONIST

Sometimes, obvious can be captivating

Sometimes too much is not even enough. While every bride is hopefully the primary focus of her wedding day, some take delight in pushing the proverbial envelope. Subtlety, intellect or art need not apply all the time. For this bride, nothing could be more glorious than a sultry, beaded wedding gown, important jewelry or an outrageous veil. What she wears clearly proclaims her sense of self and how she views the world. There is something so refreshing about such a direct and honest point of view. No matter what, the Exhibitionist is always certain to follow her own instincts. The Exhibitionist is convinced no one can ever attract too much attention.

Long-sleeved, V-neck T-shirt dress with sweep, beaded in crystal and hand-cut sequins of silver-leafed formica. *Following spread* A sleeveless "goth" full-skirted, hand-torn silk tulle coat fastened with an ivory rough-cut leather tie, over a plunging V-neck bias sleeveless chiffon gown. Beaded for Vera Wang Couture by François Lesage, Paris, France.

FABRICS, FORM AND FUNCTION

The fabric determines everything in clothing design

ANY DISCUSSION of wedding dress design begins with the fabric. In all cases, the fabric dictates the shape, drape and cut of a dress, as well as the time of day and season it can be worn. Conversely, the choice of silhouette will impact the fabric selection, as the requirements for a lavish ball gown will differ greatly from those for a narrow column. There are essentially two types of construction – structured and soft.

STRUCTURED For more conventional wedding gowns, certain fabrics have practically become generic. Stiff or substantial, these materials have the necessary body to respond in a precise way when draped. They are also ideal for fitted bodices or bustiers. The most desirable fabrics are the following: *Duchess Satin and Satin-polyester Blends* Long established as one of the most lavish and flattering materials for a formal wedding gown, satin looks important either plain or embellished. Stiff, opaque and shimmering, satin is ideal for strict A-lines, full, gathered skirts, mermaid shapes or structured bustiers. It also serves as the perfect foundation for a beautiful lace gown.

A bias strapless asymmetrical platinum Duchess satin gown worn under the sheerest layer of white mink.

Silk Taffeta, Silk Radzmere, Taffeta Blends Like Duchess satin, silk taffeta is an elegant and enduring fabric. Where satin is adaptive to both full and flat construction, taffeta looks best when gathered for volume. While taffeta comes in a wide variety of weights, textures and weaves, it is also light and airy, thus requiring a substantial foundation and multiple linings. It also rustles, so if there is even a faint possibility that this could be annoying, avoid it. Taffeta always looks most luxurious in off-white. *Satin-faced Organza* Like taffeta, satin-faced organza comes in a wide variety of weights and finishes. Lighter in appearance and less opaque than Duchess satin, this material, with its subtle, elegant, sheen, looks modern when unadorned or youthful when beaded. Thanks to its luster, organza also works beautifully in combination with other fabrics, such as lace, velvet, satin or taffeta. For sheer structure, satin-faced organza is one of my preferred fabrics.

Tulle Originally used for petticoats and underpinnings, tulle possesses a charm and beauty all its own. Tulle can be feminine, youthful and extremely versatile, whether it is draped as a simple overlay or gathered into a full-skirted ballerina gown. It can also look sleek and sculpted with a clean bodice or daring and romantic with a boned corset. I adore tulle wedding dresses any time of year. Whereas they are ideal for perching and being admired, they are far less accommodating for dancing or dining. *Brocades and Woven Jacquards* Extravagant, expensive and at times even excessive, brocades can still be extremely effective for certain formal weddings. They easily lend themselves to all types of embellishment, such as lace, embroidery, passementerie or beading. They also imply a certain bygone sense of grandeur.

A detail of a luxurious cashmere Alpaca full skirted one-shouldered wedding gown with cartridge pleating in back and hand welting on the bodice. Worn with a tip-dyed fox shrug.

Silk Faille While the thickness of faille can make it difficult to sew, like taffeta, faille is equally suited to full, extravagant shapes.

Basket Weaves Lighter and crisper than more traditional fabrics like satin-faced organza, basket weaves can be charming for less formal weddings. Modern and versatile, basket weaves work beautifully either plain or heavily embellished.

SOFT CONSTRUCTION Some brides opt for a more seductive or casual approach to wedding attire. For sheer comfort and a subtle articulation of the body, a narrow wedding gown can strike the perfect compromise between sensual and celebratory.

Silk Crepe and Crepe Blends Understated yet elegant, silk crepe continues to be popular for wedding and evening gowns alike. It is also a versatile fabric that can be worn draped and embellished or tailored and plain. A silk crepe wedding gown makes an ideal foil for elaborate accessories, special jewelry or extravagant flowers. It is also timeless and seasonless.

Silk Charmeuse Charmeuse is still one of the most glamorous and luxurious fabrics. Immortalized by the screen siren Jean Harlow, silk charmeuse was primarily used for extravagant undergarments and expensive evening gowns during the 1930s. Daring and provocative, silk charmeuse implied a certain kind of decadence normally reserved for the bedroom. Even today, it may draw unwanted attention to every nuance of the body. And due to it's shine, silk charmeuse is best worn unadorned.

A bias cut asymmetric ivory silk charmeuse mermaid gown with silk passementeries woven in Paris by Lesage for Vera Wang Couture.

Georgette A sheer, sensuous fabric, georgette drapes wonderfully. It is also more forgiving than many other fabrics and thus easier to wear than body-skimming jerseys or silk chiffon. Due to its inherent transparency, georgette requires a special lining and is most appropriate for late-day or evening ceremonies. *Silk Chiffon* Sheerer than georgette, chiffon comes in a variety of weights, finishes and transparencies. A challenging fabric to engineer, particularly when cut on the bias, chiffon has a certain implied seduction that makes it one of my personal favorites. Again, linings are a serious factor due to the fabric's sheerness. *Jerseys, from Matte to Wool* For the fashion-forward bride, few fabrics are as seductive as matte jersey. Long before stretch fabrics were ever invented, jerseys supplied the necessary give and drape for body-conscious gowns. While silk and matte jerseys are appropriate any time of year, wool jersey is always an elegant alternative for a winter reception. *Velvets; Cotton, Silk Panné, Washed, Burn-out and Blends* While velvet is ideal for certain afternoon or late-day ceremonies, it is rarely worn today for weddings. Whether it is fashioned into a stiff, traditional bodice or a soft narrow column, silk velvet can look ravishing in white, ivory or the palest hint of color, regardless of the season. *Stretch Illusion* Stretch illusion, another signature fabric of mine, is not only comfortable to wear, but incredibly flattering. It is also versatile as an accent or as an entire gown.

A Roman-inspired toga dress in luxurious ivory silk velvet with full bias sleeves, a knotted front and a puddling train.

ON LACE

Fragile and timeless

ONCE CHERISHED as the ultimate wedding fabric because of its intrinsic delicacy, scarcity and cost, lace is no longer as popular as it once was. For the bride who wishes to embrace tradition, however, nothing says more about weddings than lace. While there are infinite varieties of lace, each specific weave has it's own distinct look and defining characteristics. The range in styles is enormous, from fragile and delicate chantilly lace, to elaborate reembroidered Alençon or Venise. Lace is particularly well-suited for morning or day-time weddings, as it provides adornment and texture without beading or shine. When coupled with other delicate fabrics such as silk taffeta or Duchess satin, lace can provide just the right amount of tradition.

ELEMENTS OF DESIGN

EACH COMPONENT OF A WEDDING GOWN DESERVES EQUAL ATTENTION. NO DECISION REGARDING STYLE OR SHAPE CAN BE MADE UNTIL THE BRIDE HAS DETERMINED WHICH PHYSICAL ATTRIBUTES SHE WOULD LIKE TO EMPHASIZE.

NECKLINES From a cultural and historical perspective, necklines, like hemlines, possess enormous style significance. They also provide great visual impact and the perfect frame for a bride's face, shoulders and breasts. THERE ARE THREE CATEGORIES of necklines, each of which infers a different style of gown and bodice. Whereas a bodice delineates the torso, a neckline emphasizes the bosom. Because a neckline and bodice are both integral to the overall design, they also define the look and fit of a gown.

ON-THE-SHOULDER An on-the-shoulder neckline is always engineered with armholes or shoulder straps. This affords the necessary coverage for bras and bra straps while allowing for a certain freedom of arm movement, when desired.

NECKLINES AND BODICES
Too obvious is seldom appropriate

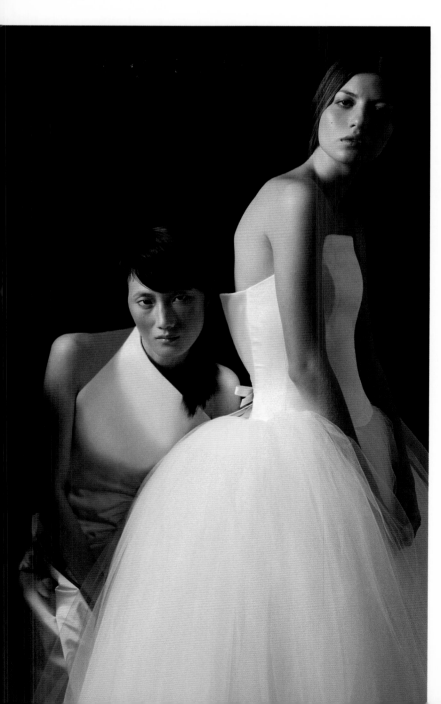

OFF-THE-SHOULDER OR PORTRAIT A portrait or off-the-shoulder neckline is a feminine shape that is flattering on most brides. While this style focuses enormous attention on the face and shoulders, a portrait neckline can also be highly restrictive. If dancing is a major consideration, the singular glamour of a portrait neckline might have to be sacrificed in favor of a more versatile shape.

STRAPLESS Strapless necklines are enjoying an enormous resurgence, not only because they are evocative of the 1950s, but because many brides prefer to expose more skin. Bare yet refined, romantic but dignified, a strapless neckline strikes the perfect balance between propriety and flirtation.

BODICES Each component of a traditional wedding gown depends on the design of the bodice. Like a foundation garment, a bodice is defined by its construction and fit. Regardless of shape, fabric or design, a bodice must be tailored precisely to the length of the torso. As strapless bodices require stays for structure and support, it is crucial that the overall proportions be correct for maximum comfort.

FOR THE FULLER BOSOM ▪ For a short-waisted figure, the fitter should add extra stays for support, particularly to the center front. ▪ To create an illusion of length, a bodice should extend a bit lower onto the torso. ▪ Excessive drape, fabric or ornamentation always add unnecessary volume to a full bosom. ▪ Undergarments and linings

For many women, sensuality is expressed through the choice of neckline and bodice. *Left* An asymmetrical Duchess satin gown and a strapless tulle ballerina gown with inverted back center pleat. *Opposite* Sexy yet discreet. A modern take on a crumb-catcher bodice with bias straps that gently twist onto the shoulder. A grosgrain of ivory silk wraps around the waist and through the neckline into a tailored bow.

must be skillfully engineered for an unconstructed gown. Without the proper foundation, a bias cut, body-skimming slip dress will definitely create support issues. ▪ An additional layer of stretch lining may be necessary to prevent sagging. ▪ If a conventional bra is needed, the bodice of the gown, too, must have shoulder straps.

FOR A SMALL BOSOM ▪ A deep V-neck can be flattering while a high neckline always looks elegant. ▪ A carved racer-front or narrow halter can look sleek and sexy on a small bosom. ▪ For a corseted bodice, the cup size must be correct. All the youthful charm of a smaller chest will be lost on an ill-fitting bustier. ▪ Thin bare tops are usually more flattering on small-breasted women.

FOR ALL SIZES ▪ Excessive padding in the bust area always looks artificial. ▪ Beware of fitters who fill-in the bodice with extra bust pads to avoid making the necessary alterations. ▪ The crumb-catcher — an outer layer of fabric that encases the bodice — always enhances a small bust line, while providing additional support for a full one. ▪ Even for a night-time wedding, obvious décolleté is never appropriate for the ceremony.

GENERAL TIPS ON NECKLINES ▪ When choosing a neckline, a bride should consider her weight, height, bone structure and age. The smaller the bride, the shorter she will look with a décolleté; the older the bride, the less she should reveal. ▪ A clean, athletic neckline such as a bib, racer or halter makes even the fullest gown look sleek and sculpted. ▪ Stretch illusion or sheer fabrics like silk net, chiffon or lace are flattering on women of all ages. ▪ Sheer fabric always makes a high neckline look more seductive. ▪ Necklines should be discreet for a morning ceremony, while late-day and evening celebrations allow for more latitude. ▪ Even a high neckline can be provocative with an element of surprise such as a plunging back.

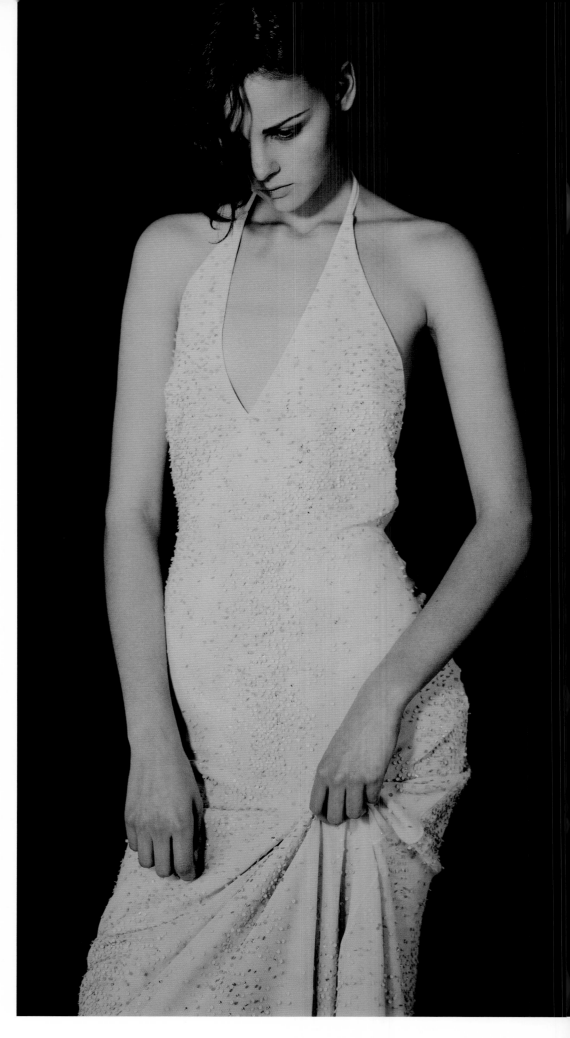

Above A plunging V-halter neckline in delicate silk georgette graces a bias cut mermaid gown embroidered entirely with tiny leather sequins and crystals. *Opposite* Another take on a classic crumb-catcher bodice, this time with contoured straps and horizontal gathers. The sleek proportion of the A-line skirt is further emphasized by the voluminous detachable pouf sleeves.

THE EFFECT OF A SLEEVE or armhole on the design of a dress should never be under-estimated. The shape, volume and length of a sleeve should be determined by the bride's specific proportions. While the perfect sleeve can enhance a gown or downplay difficult arms, the wrong one will compromise the design of the dress and the look of the bride. The proportion of an armhole will always impact the construction of the sleeve and neckline.

NARROW, STRAIGHT SLEEVES

From long or wrist-length to elbow, three-quarter or bracelet-length, sleeves have again become extremely popular. Elegant and modern or slightly retro, narrow sleeves naturally lend themselves to such decorative details as ruffles, buttons, trims or slits. AN ELBOW-LENGTH SLEEVE complements the style-conscious bride who also desires coverage. Long, narrow sleeves can be flattering and fashion

ON SLEEVES

A sleeve can be a style consideration or a necessity

forward when cut out of a soft fabric. Long sleeves can even look seductive when constructed from thin transparent materials such as lace, chiffon, silk net or stretch illusion. The shorter the sleeve, the more youthful the look. In fact, tiny sleeves can often be harder to wear than no sleeves at all.

WIDE SLEEVES

A DOLMAN SLEEVE is wide at the armhole, tapering to a narrow bottom. As the dolman emphasizes the shoulder and arm, it can be quite dramatic in a soft fabric like jersey. A KIMONO SLEEVE is cut in a wide rectangle from a dropped shoulder. Like a dolman, a kimono sleeve is visually distinctive.

FULL SLEEVES

A TINY POUF or Juliette sleeve is even more extreme than a cap sleeve. Perfect arms, however, are a prerequisite. Often paired with an empire waistline and a low décolleté, this silhouette places great emphasis on the bosom. Again, it is a decidedly youthful look for the most fashion-savvy bride. A BALLOON OR POUF SLEEVE is often constructed of light, pliable fabrics like taffeta or radzmere. This style also works well in Duchess satin or soft, transparent fabrics like chiffon or georgette. A full pouf sleeve can conceal problem arms.

SLEEVELESS

The sleeveless gown is a signature look for me. Timeless, chic and sophisticated, a sleeveless dress is extremely practical for dancing and highlights great arms.

Above left A detachable silk faille sleeve on a modern version of a French court dress. *Opposite A* silk georgette mermaid gown with a front cowl neckline and detachable bias cut chiffon sleeves. *Above* Illustration of the sleeve detail in photograph above left.

While a neckline and bodice frame a bride's face, neck and shoulders, the shape and positioning of the waistline will determine the overall silhouette of her gown. For many, the waist is a bride's best asset and deserves great emphasis.

■ An empire waist is a seam tucked just under the bosom. ■ A high-waist is positioned anywhere across the rib cage, roughly two inches above the natural waistline. Like an empire waist, this proportion creates an illusion of long legs. It is also an extremely flattering proportion for most brides. ■ A natural waistline is a seam placed directly at the actual waist. Reminiscent of styles of the 1950s, it works best on a narrow or A-line skirt. ■ A basque waistline is comprised of two curved seams that form a "V" just below the natural waistline. A basque waist can be carved to any proportion. While flattering on most women, a basque must be adjusted to the individual. The bodice will only fit properly if the waistline is placed at just the right height. ■ Kidney-shaped or S-shaped waistlines are also flattering. The "S" shape is created by a seam that dips center-front then curves gently up over the hips. Like a basque, this shape creates the illusion of a long torso and a narrow waist.

WAISTLINES

A waistline is key to the fit of a gown

■ A trapezoid-shaped waistline has a horizontal seam that rises sharply at an angle on both sides. More geometric than an "S" waistline, a trapezoid waist achieves much the same effect as a basque or kidney-shaped seam. ■ A high-to-low waistline is a gently curved seam that rises center-front and eventually dips down at the sides. ■ Original and unconventional, an asymmetric or off-center waistline makes a bold design statement in soft or stiff fabrications. The asymmetry eventually effects the drape of the bustle in back. ■ The dropped waist, as its name implies, is any horizontal seam that sits well below the waistline. When worn two to three inches beneath the natural waist, a dropped waistline also creates the illusion of a long torso. ■ The princess shape consists of two vertical seams that taper to the hem without any seams at the waist. Because a princess shape is elongating, it also flatters a wide variety of figure types.

Left A thin belt articulates the natural waistline in this illustration of a narrow-to-full skirted wedding gown. *Opposite* A soft strapless gown fashioned out of layers of sheer satin-faced organza, embroidered with giant ferns of antique silver bouillon thread. A narrow tie of Duchess satin is elegantly knotted at the waist.

Above Victoria Beckham wears a gently shaped S-waistline that clearly emphasizes the narrowness of the torso and the volume of the crumb-catcher bodice. Foundation bodice by Mr. Pearl for Vera Wang. *Opposite* A detail of a modified strapless sweetheart neckline with a basque waist. From the delicate bra cups to the curve of the bodice, each kind of stitching helps to articulate the waist.

Left A muslin of a structured bias cut mermaid skirt with multi-layered hemlines. *Below* A muslin of a classic A-line strapless wedding gown. This shape is flattering on most brides. *Opposite* An ivory strapless satin-faced organza bias wedding gown with a raised waistseam and layered hemline. Worn with a silk tulle veiling that cascades into a train.

SKIRTS

Shape determines design

SKIRT DESIGN While shape and fabric determine the look of a dress, the drape and detail of the skirt define the outcome. From hand-pleating to petal-backs, side-drapes to side-swags, curved seams to layered hems, the design of a skirt provides volume, surface interest and movement. It's silhouette always effects the style of a wedding gown.

SHAPES

FULL An enormous gathered skirt always makes a grand and glorious impression. And a wedding presents one of the rare occasions on which to wear such an extravagant silhouette. The volume of the skirt should be determined by the formality of the wedding and the proportions of the bride. While a full gown can create the semblance of a narrow waist or offset an ample bosom, this silhouette can be overwhelming on a petite bride.

A-LINE An A-line shape is always elongating. A-lines reflect not only a classic sense of refinement but an inherent love of form. Worn full, an A-line can be extravagant without sacrificing slimness, while a narrow A-line can be either dressy or informal. Remember, an A-line can only be bustled if the skirt has enough volume in back. Otherwise, the train must be detachable. This versatile shape also helps to minimize a heavy figure.

Left A pair of bias cut silk charmeuse evening gowns hand-embroidered with lace appliqués and lattice work of satin strips. *Opposite* A strapless wedding gown with an extravagant circular skirt of ivory satin-faced organza veiled in silk tulle.

CIRCULAR A circular skirt has great fullness and movement. Stylistically, it is best suited for a tall, thin frame. When constructed out of a stiff fabric like satin-faced organza, a circular gown can be quite grand. In soft fabrics like chiffon, it can be incredibly graceful.
MERMAID A mermaid shape clearly articulates the curves of the body. Ideal for an afternoon or evening wedding, it also suits a wide variety of body types. Elongating on small women and extremely flattering on full ones, the outright sexiness of a mermaid may necessitate a cover-up, particularly for a more conservative ceremony. Like a narrow column or an A-line gown, a mermaid cannot be bustled. For more daring brides, the appeal of such a body-conscious shape clearly compensates for the wear and tear of a dragging hem.
NARROW COLUMNS A floor-length sheath or shift provides a sophisticated alternative to a full gown. Short and tailored or long, slinky and bare, this obvious evening wear shape is still considered surprisingly avant-garde for a wedding gown.
ASYMMETRICAL Unexpected and often difficult to wear, an asymmetrical shape can make a bold statement for the less conventional bride.
BALLOON OR POUF Short or long, a balloon skirt is a full, gathered shape that tapers slightly at the hemline. A short pouf with a dropped waistline can appear to elongate a short torso. It can also create sufficient volume to minimize a broad waist or heavy legs.

Above An ivory Duchess satin strapless modified mermaid gown with a matching A-line detachable overskirt. *Opposite* An ivory sheer organza halter gown with delicate bias cut satin concentric ribbon borders.

NARROW TO FULL For brides who want the extravagance of a full silhouette for the ceremony but desire a slimmer shape for the reception, a removable train or detachable overskirt offers a practical compromise.

LENGTHS Although most brides opt for a floor-length hemline, there are countless alternative lengths. Short lengths emphasize great legs while short-to-long hemlines only look good on a tall, narrow silhouette. As a rule of thumb, the more formal the ceremony, the longer the hemline.

MINI For women who are youthful and possess incredible legs, a mini dress can be a fun and frivolous choice for an informal ceremony or a stylish cocktail reception. To offset the bareness, a long coat or floor-length detachable overskirt can provide an elegant, dignified counterpoint.

JUST-BELOW-THE-KNEE Equally ideal for a chic cocktail dress or a stylish dinner suit, this traditional length is appropriate for all but the most formal of weddings. It, too, flatters many different figure types and is well suited for women of all ages.

"CHANEL" LENGTH A finger-length below the knee, or "chanel" length, is one of my preferred lengths for a coat and dress ensemble or a sexy, beaded slip dress. Less conventional than just-below-the-knee, this hemline is always graceful and stylish, if not a bit eccentric.

MID-CALF HEMLINE Depending upon the shape and volume, a mid-calf length can be either severe or poetic. This hemline is best worn with low to medium heels for an informal wedding. Sometimes a full ballerina silhouette requires a high neckline to offset the volume of the skirt.

ANKLE LENGTH Longer than mid-calf yet shorter than floor-length, this hem is ideal for less formal weddings, particularly when paired with low-heeled mules or sandals. An ankle-length can be uniquely feminine in a full silhouette or sleek and modern in a narrow one.

SHORT-TO-LONG Hemlines that graduate from short to long focus enormous attention on the lower leg and ankles. This rather unconventional silhouette requires long legs and significant height. While I adore this concept, it is a difficult proportion on most women.

ARBITRARY Like asymmetrical and uneven hemlines, strange or unusual hem lengths only flatter women with extremely long legs.

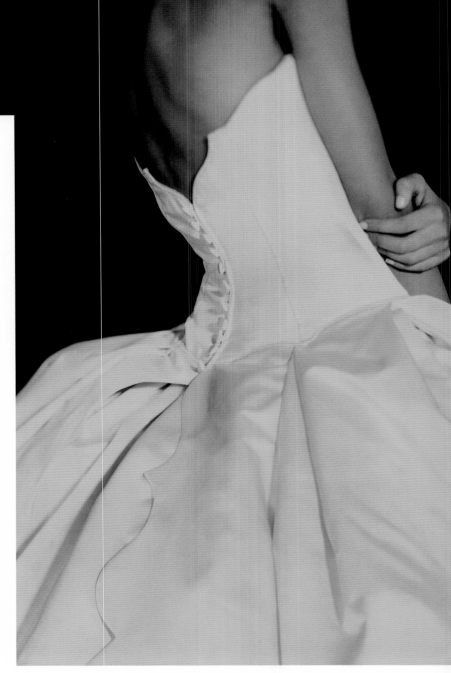

THE BACK

A different perspective

AS THE BACK of a wedding gown commands its own share of visual importance during the ceremony, it is crucial that the gown be conceived with this unique perspective in mind. The charm of an artfully designed back lies in a confluence of cut, drape and decoration, with such significant details as intricate seaming or complex construction.

MORNING CEREMONIES always dictate a special measure of propriety. As such, the back of a gown should never sit below the level of the bra fastening. Traditional wedding adornments such as tailored bows, fabric-covered buttons or hand-rolled flowers lend a touch of subtle femininity and grace to the back of a bodice.

FOR LATE-DAY OR EVENING WEDDINGS, more embellishment is always appropriate, if not desirable. A glimpse of bare skin or the soft drape of a cowl-back can both be incredibly alluring, while sequins, beads and crystals reflect light and offer a touch of glamour.

AS SOME BRIDES FAVOR a more tailored look, a clean architectural back merits important design consideration. A sheer panel, perhaps of stretch illusion, can provide a bit of intrigue for a more sedate gown.

ANY DRESSMAKING DETAILS such as ruching, gathers, twists or folds can add great drama and importance to the back of a gown. So can delicate stitching, tiny pin-tucks or a pair of gently carved shoulder straps. Beaded or jeweled straps also provide a certain sensual dimension on a bare back. Decoration need not only be restricted to the front of a wedding gown.

Left A Grecian-inspired plunging tie-back ivory crepe gown. *Below* A structured strapless full-skirted Duchess satin gown with square fabric-covered buttons and hand-carved edges. *Opposite* An ivory strapless full-skirted silk-faille wedding gown with a split-back bodice fastened with black satin hand-tied bows.

Left Strapless silk faille A-line dress with twisted back that falls into an empire train. *Above* Bias silk crepe strapless dress with lace-up back. *Opposite* Strapless full pouf dress of silk radzmere with square buttons and knotted fringed bow.

TRAINS AND BUSTLES

A lot of pomp and circumstance

THERE ARE TWO CATEGORIES OF TRAINS, each with its own distinct advantages and disadvantages.

THE INTEGRATED OR ATTACHED TRAIN An integrated train is conceived as part of the gown and must be bustled.

THERE ARE THREE VARIATIONS
BUSTLE A bustle is achieved by lifting up the fabric of the train and fastening it to the rest of the dress with delicate buttons and loops, tiny hooks and eyes or snaps. For the bride's sense of security, it is vital that all the stitching details be carefully reinforced on the skirt. It is also important that the bustling procedure be rehearsed several times. The versatility of an integrated bustle becomes most apparent after the ceremony, when the bride needs to maneuver comfortably among her guests. Be advised, however, that the weight and dimension of a bustle might add unwanted volume to the backside.

FINGER LOOPS For some shapes, like narrow A-lines that cannot be bustled, a finger loop serves as a functional style alternative. A delicate loop of thread is attached to the center-back hem of the gown, enabling the bride to lift the excess fabric off the floor by slipping her finger through the loop. A skirt must be specifically engineered, however, to be worn in this manner.

Above Back view of a muslin for a full-skirted gown, ideal for a more theatrical bride. *Opposite* A petal-shaped back with Moorish-inspired scalloping in stone-colored Duchess satin. *Previous pages left* Silk zibeline structured A-line dress with detachable empire train. *Right* Bias silk chiffon halter dress with detachable ruched train.

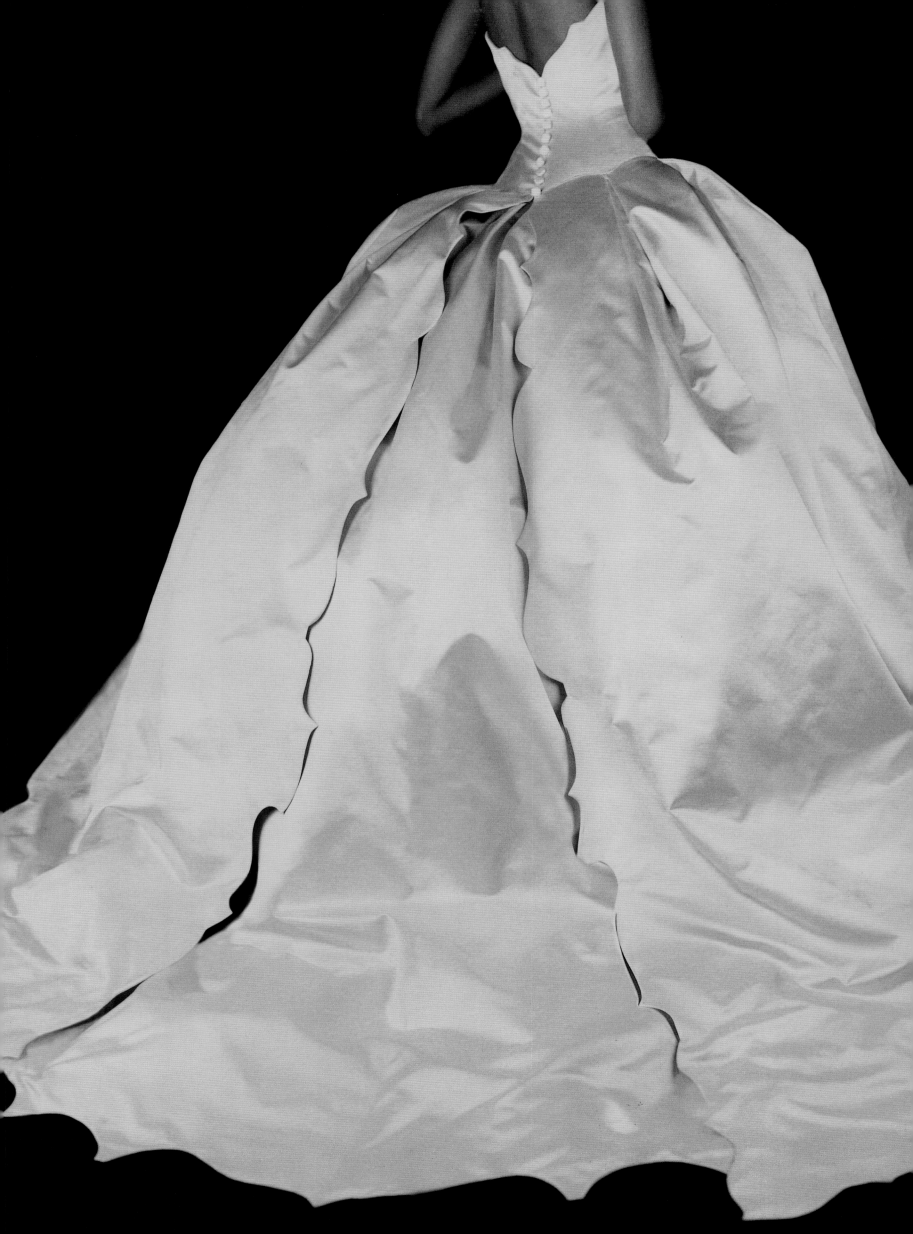

CARRIED Like a cathedral veil, an extended train must be gathered up from the floor and draped over the arm. This graceful gesture is also a practical way to manage the train after the ceremony. Again, the skirt should be deliberately engineered to be worn in this manner.

THE DETACHED OR REMOVABLE TRAIN

THERE ARE TWO TYPES of detachable trains. One is fastened to the back of the gown while the other is worn as a completely separate overskirt. For the bride who appreciates the splendor of a full-skirted gown at the ceremony but longs for the seduction of a narrow silhouette at the reception, a detachable train can offer the ideal compromise. Both versions may be either bustled or discarded after the wedding service. Regardless, a detachable or removable train should always reflect the shape of the dress underneath.

DETACHABLE OR NOT, all trains may be fastened to various points on a dress, starting at the nape of the neck.

STYLES OF TRAINS

THE WATTEAU The Watteau train is sewn across the back of the shoulders, then gathered into folds that fall to the floor and sweep into a train. Due to its intrinsic grandeur, a Watteau can look extremely impressive, but also a touch theatrical. Watteau trains still enjoy some degree of popularity in Europe. For the sake of convenience, they need to be detachable for after the ceremony.

THE EMPIRE Attached just below the shoulder blades and trailing down to the floor, an empire train is far less overbearing than a Watteau. Like most trains and bustles, an empire shape always dignifies the back of a wedding gown. It is also equally graceful in either soft or stiff fabrications.

THE NATURAL This is often a difficult silhouette for someone with an ample bosom or a short midriff because of the extra emphasis it places at the waist. It is a silhouette, however, that infers a timeless sense of style.

Opposite A rigid cowl-back bias mermaid gown with extended sweep and tailored bows at the neckline.

THE LENGTH OF THE TRAIN

INTEGRATED OR DETACHABLE TRAINS can be cut to any length. The more formal the gown, the longer the train.

FLOOR-LENGTH Always appropriate, particularly for less formal weddings, a floor-length train should fall precisely to the ground. It is an ideal length for petite brides.

THE SWEEP A sweep extends out about one foot from the body. It always creates a graceful and romantic finish. Like a godet, a sweep is more of an embellishment than a structural element.

THE CHAPEL Depending on the height of the bride, a chapel train should extend six to eight feet from her waist or three to four feet behind her. Classic yet elegant, the chapel is surprisingly easy to manage yet considerably more emphatic than shorter lengths. Suitable for small brides or more formal ceremonies, a chapel train always makes an important wedding statement.

THE CATHEDRAL A cathedral train extends nine feet from the waist and deserves a venue of equally majestic scale. It can be worn with any type of veil but combines best with one of similar proportions. Due to its extreme length, a cathedral is difficult to negotiate when moving in any direction other than a straight line.

THE ROYAL As its name implies, the royal train should be worn for only the most formal weddings. Absurd in any context other than a state or royal ceremony, a royal train usually extends twenty-five feet from the waistline. Needless to say, it takes several attendants to maneuver a royal train.

Opposite A pair of Grecian-inspired column gowns with integrated trains.

THE AMOUNT OF ADORNMENT on a gown should reflect the tenor of the celebration as well as the shape of the dress.

THERE ARE TWO kinds of ornamentation — decoration that is added on and decorative details that are engineered into the gown. These can be used either separately or in conjunction with one another.

ADDED

PIPINGS, TRIMS, BORDERS AND EDGES From the thinnest, most delicate edges, like sutash and hand-rolled chiffon piping, to bias cut satin borders, silk grosgrain ribbons, woven passementeries and hand-pieced lace trims, this category of decoration can be used to accentuate a hemline, the shape of a waistline or any manner of seaming. For greater emphasis, borders and trims can be beaded.

HANDMADE BOWS, CLOCARDS AND SILK OR HAND-ROLLED FLOWERS Especially becoming on more youthful or naive wedding gowns, these decorative details can conceal the hooks on a bustle or enhance the straps of a bodice. They are also effective for daytime weddings, when some adornment is desirable but beading is inappropriate.

ORNAMENTATION

To bead or not to bead

SASHES AND TIES An extravagant sash trailing down the back of a gown provides a romantic detail or a touch of drama.

BUTTONS AND FASTENINGS From delicate lingerie hooks to tiny, fabric-covered buttons and loops, these elements comprise some of the most traditional and timeless details on a wedding gown.

ENGINEERED

EMBROIDERY Hand-embroidered details, though costly, add importance and visual excitement to most traditional wedding gowns. From threads of silk, cotton or wool, to metal bouillon in gold, silver or bronze, intricate hand embroidery presents an elegant alternative to flashy beads.

BEADING Beading is most effective on wedding gowns in delicate floral motifs, subtle abstract patterns or decorative borders. Some of the most beautiful materials are hand-cut Italian sequins, crystals, faceted beads, baroque pearls or semiprecious stones.

HAND PAINTING Imaginative and original, hand painting is one of my favorite techniques. Whether it's a single flower or an all-over design, nothing is more subtle or expressive than painting on fabric.

SOME CONSIDERATIONS ▪ Pearls are the most appropriate form of beading for a morning ceremony. ▪ It is always best to avoid inexpensive beading. ▪ The most extraordinary gown can be ruined by garish beading or excessive ornamentation.

Opposite A bias cut satin back crepe halter gown with jeweled straps by Lesage for Vera Wang Couture.

Opposite Heavy reembroidered lace provides texture and ornamentation when fashioned into a wedding gown devoid of all decoration. *Left* A bias gossamer silk tulle wedding gown hand-embroidered with flowers of delicate ribbon offers a poetic alternative to a structured ball gown. *Above* A strapless satin-faced organza mermaid gown evokes yet another take on modern wedding beading. Worn with a matching chiffon bolero, this is a perfect look for a bride who prefers to mix sensuality with propriety.

THERE IS NOTHING QUITE AS TRANSFORMATIONAL as a bridal veil. Other than the wedding ring, it is perhaps the most symbolic accessory a woman will ever wear. The "donning" of the veil is a wedding custom that exists in nearly every culture around the world. It is also a ritual with enduring social and religious implications and one to which many brides still subscribe.

THE CHOICE OF VEIL depends upon many considerations.
■ The nature of the celebration ■ The bride's features and facial structure ■ The bride's height frame ■ The style of the gown ■ The length of the train ■ The bride's hairstyle ■ The bridal headpiece, if any ■ The location ■ The dimensions of the aisle ■ The weather, particularly the wind factor

SHAPE
THE GATHERED OR POUF VEIL A gathered veil can be fashioned to any length or with any amount of fullness. The more gathers, the more volume and the more opaque the look. ■ A veil that is too dense will photograph poorly. ■ While a gathered veil is dramatic, it can overwhelm a small face or petite bride.

THE WEDDING VEIL
Sacred yet seductive

■ A gathered veil, however, can offset an extremely full silhouette or a bride who is heavyset. ■ A gathered veil is most beautiful when fastened to the crown of the head. ■ A pouf veil can be worn with a blusher separately or attached.

THE PETAL OR CAGE VEIL Short and slightly gathered or flat and circular, a petal veil is split down the center front with a square or rounded edge. It looks equally charming with a tailored suit, a cocktail dress or a formal wedding gown.
FOR THE BRIDE WHO must cover her head for religious reasons, but hesitates to wear a long veil, a cage is the perfect compromise. Sometimes, after the ceremony, a bride will switch from a long veil to a petal veil for the reception. Because the veil is so short — most often it grazes around the shoulder or above — it is best to avoid trims of any kind.

CIRCULAR OR DROPPED VEIL Unlike a gathered veil, a dropped veil is a flat piece of tulle that is quite literally dropped onto the bride's head then secured with a comb and hairpins. It creates volume but no height. Sheer and sensuous, a floor-length dropped veil emphasizes the bride's silhouette. In addition to a circular shape, variations on a dropped veil might be oval, square or rectangle. ■ A dropped veil is far more streamlined than a pouf. ■ Worn over a headpiece, a dropped veil adds drama and importance. ■ A dropped veil worn under a headpiece looks subtle and graceful. ■ For volume, a dropped veil can be layered with a gathered veil. ■ While a dropped veil can be fastened anywhere on the head, when pinned at the nape of the neck, it creates a slightly nonchalant effect.

Opposite A satin bias slip dress with hand-embroidered lace appliqués and latticework of bias cut satin strips. A skullcap of Lyon lace and a chapel-length, square-cut dropped veil. The blend of sensuality and ritual is positively seductive.

Portrait by Paolo Roversi

MANTILLA A mantilla is a dropped veil that is often fashioned out of lace and is sometimes antique. It is fastened anywhere to the crown. It can provide a decorative counterpoint to an unadorned gown.

BLUSHERS Whether it is the portion of the veil that falls forward and covers the face or a completely separate entity, a blusher adds enormous dignity and mystery to a conventional veil. While a blusher may be too theatrical for some brides, for others it can be quite compelling. Like the veil itself, the blusher can be worn to any length in front, from the chin to the floor. The blusher should never be cut with gathers that could cast shadows across a bride's face.

LENGTHS

ANY LENGTH OF VEIL is appropriate for a wedding and each variation impacts the proportions of the face differently.
■ CHIN TO SHOULDER Perfect for cage or petal shapes. ■ ELBOW LENGTH Classic, demure, reminiscent and slightly retro. ■ BOUQUET Meant to cover or clear the bouquet in front, depending on the bride's proportions. ■ FINGERTIP More exaggerated than an elbow-length, it is a chic and unusual proportion on a tall bride. ■ FLOOR LENGTH Impeccable when worn with a gown of precisely the same length. ■ SWEEP A veil with the same dimensions as those of a sweep train. Graceful yet manageable, it can be the perfect length for a petite bride or a less formal ceremony. ■ CHAPEL The chapel veil is cut to the exact same proportions as a chapel train, in either a gathered or dropped shape. ■ CATHEDRAL Due to its length, a cathedral veil lends itself equally to more ornate decoration or utter simplicity. ■ ROYAL The longest veil by far, a royal length veil should only be worn by royalty. *Although I cite all traditional veil lengths, I generally adhere to my own sense of proportion when working with clients, trusting my eye rather than relying on standard measurements.*

DECORATION

Any decoration on a veil, particularly wide trims or heavy lace appliqués, will overwhelm most brides. Despite the temptation to over-embellish, a certain discipline should always be maintained where ornamentation is concerned.
■ Even sutash piping may be too much detail on a small frame. ■ Any narrow ribbon or bias cut trim looks tailored and elegant for a daytime wedding. Make sure the width of the trim is proportionate to the face and height of the bride. ■ For a morning wedding, delicate pearl trim can be a chic alternative to beading. Scattered pearls or rhinestones are only appropriate at night. ■ Any trim that picks up a specific detail of the dress can be subtle and elegant. Velvet trims always work particularly well for a fall or winter wedding. ■ For evening, miniature silk flowers with jeweled centers can be scattered over the entire veil or worn as a trim along the edge. ■ A hand-embroidered veil is always a true extravagance. ■ For evening weddings, beading can be an intriguing way to add luminosity to a bride's face. *Lace is one of the ultimate luxuries, particularly when it is passed down from generation to generation. For those who anticipate wearing an heirloom veil, it should be brought to each shopping appointment.*

Opposite A frothy confection of hand-crafted silk tulle can serve not only as a magnificent headcovering, but as a seductive and unconventional wedding veil.

THE BRIDAL HEADPIECE

The crowning touch

BEFORE CHOOSING A HEADDRESS, consider the veil, gown and hairstyle. Since these elements are interrelated, the wrong hair ornament or headpiece could detract from the bride's overall appearance. The decorative impact of a headpiece should never be underestimated, whether it is worn with a veil or on its own.

TIARA OR JEWELED HEADBAND Worn casually with a modern gown or as a complement to a fanciful dress, a tiara can be positively magical. However, it requires enormous personal style to wear a tiara effectively. Due to its implied grandeur, a tiara is not suitable for all weddings. The proportions of the tiara must also correspond to the bride's physiognomy — while an excessively wide tiara will overwhelm delicate features, a tiara with great height will definitely elongate the face.

FLOWERS Whether they are freshly cut and carefully arranged in a bride's hair minutes before the ceremony or handmade and jeweled to match the dress, flowers provide their own sense of femininity. They also provide the perfect material for fashioning a crown or headband. As always, scale is important, whether it's a single blossom or an entire wreath. Worn with or without a veil, a floral wreath can serve as the perfect complement to the bride's bouquet or a floral detail on her gown.

BOWS, BARRETTES, COMBS AND PINS An elegant bow is a tailored look for a conservative daytime wedding. To achieve a similar effect for an evening event, a bow encrusted with tiny pearls or stones is appropriate. All manner of decorative hair ornaments such as jeweled barrettes, elaborate combs or delicate hairpins can be incorporated into any hairstyle for a late-day or evening wedding, if so desired.

HATS With just enough charm to be frivolous and flirtatious, hats recall eras past. As with veils and headpieces, a hat should be chosen with the gown and the hairdo in mind. ▪ Be aware of the season when choosing the fabrication of a hat; organdy, straw and silk are all elegant alternatives for a spring or a summer ceremony, while wool felt, fur or velvet can be sumptuous for fall and winter. ▪ For a petite bride, smaller brims and less volume are always more flattering. ▪ There is no more appropriate occasion for a stylish hat than a daytime ceremony, as most daytime wedding services require some form of headwear. Nothing is more captivating than a wide-brimmed straw hat with an impeccably tailored suit.

CAPS With or without a veil, a skullcap always creates the illusion of a diminutive head shape. Whether it is fashioned out of lace or taffeta or embellished with beading, piping or hand-embroidery, it can complement delicate features or accentuate strong ones.

Above A garland of English ivy represents a wonderfully pagan symbol of marriage. *Overlay* A handmade silk tulle Juliette cap embellished with tiny delicate crystals by Swarovski. *Opposite* Diamond and platinum art deco tiara worn with diamond and platinum art deco earrings, circa 1910. Fred Leighton, New York City.

Portraits by Paolo Roversi

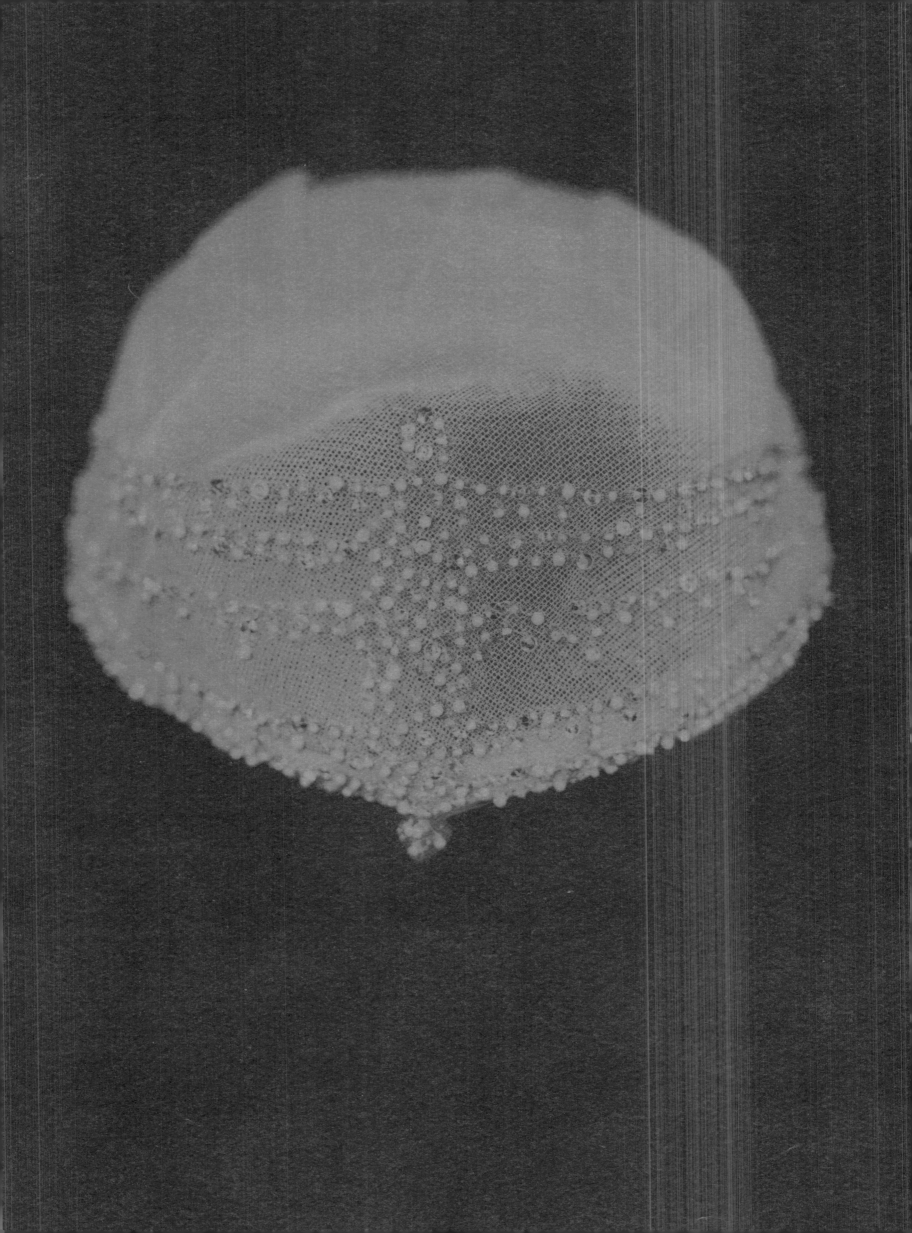

COVER-UPS AND CONVERTIBLES

A look for every whim

Yvonne Force and Leo Villareal, November 14, 1998, 5pm, private residence, Cuernavaca, Mexico.

GIVEN THE CONTEMPORARY BRIDE'S PENCHANT for bareness, cover-ups have become a significant ceremony consideration. For a highly religious wedding service or a more conservative celebration, some additional element of clothing may be required for the appropriate amount of coverage. Certain cover-ups and clothing separates also provide a clever excuse for a change of attire. Brides who opt for an entirely different look after the ceremony and seek a versatile piece of clothing can create a whole other mood with the addition of a cover-up or a convertible. A tiny jeweled bolero, a detachable overskirt or a graceful georgette coat are all fashion pieces that offer a subtle shift in style or a complete change of silhouette.
■ A Duchess satin wedding gown looks incredibly glamorous when accessorized with a matching wrap. ■ A fur shrug or scarf can winterize a satin-faced organza gown. ■ Matching elements of clothing such as a tailored coat or jacket can provide an entirely different look when worn over a feminine wedding gown. ■ Sheer georgette pieces offer just the right amount of coverage for a bare gown. ■ A cashmere hooded floor-length cape can be a practical and luxurious cover-up for a winter wedding, as can a featherweight, fur-lined opera coat. ■ A split-front detachable overskirt transforms a narrow bias column into a full ball gown.

WHILE THE ALLURE OF A GARTER BELT, sheer stockings and a thong is irresistible for some brides, sexy undergarments are hardly the most comfortable foundation for the longest and busiest day of one's life. The fit and fall of a wedding gown will greatly depend on the choice of underpinnings. ▪ Fit the gown with the same foundation garments each time. ▪ A narrow clingy gown will require a very different kind of undergarment than a full structured one. The same applies to a strapless dress. ▪ The solution to most fit issues is a plain, smooth undergarment with maximum support and minimal frills. ▪ If there are issues of transparency, sleek nude-colored undergarments are usually most effective. ▪ Even under a white gown, the safest color to wear is a shade darker than one's skin tone. ▪ Frilly underwear notwithstanding, consider any undergarment as a foundation for the gown rather than as a wedding accoutrement. ▪ Even a stray bra strap can ruin the look of the most perfect bride. ▪ Regarding linings and undergarments, peace of mind is a central issue to the wedding day.

THE FOUNDATION
What lies beneath

THE BRA As a strapless bra is often impractical for the full-chested bride, this should be factored into the choice of gown. Also, make sure the neckline of the dress conceals the bra straps. ▪ Heavy brides should beware of long-line bras. As bones and stays have a tendency to cut into the body, the length of the bodice is extremely critical. ▪ If the gown already has a boned bodice built in, wearing an additional one can add inches to the torso. ▪ All bras should be seamless and elasticized for a smooth line under the gown. ▪ Always bring an extra bra, in case one gets misplaced.

THE SLIP A slip can improve the appearance of almost any gown. ▪ A thin slip of synthetic fibers can help a gown skim the body. ▪ A slip with a bit of elastic woven in can also work as a full-length girdle. Always choose a slip one size larger than usual to prevent it from riding up. ▪ The silhouette and neckline of the slip should conform exactly to the cut of the gown. ▪ If a skin-colored slip feels less bridal, choose a shade of white or ivory that approximates the color of the lining of the dress.

THE PETTICOAT For lavish ball gowns or grand A-lines, the structure of the petticoat is fundamental to the shape and construction of a gown. Many brides even choose to wear a second petticoat for further emphasis. ▪ Although petticoats can be purchased in a range of volumes and lengths, most high-quality wedding gowns have their own petticoats already built into the garment. ▪ While an additional petticoat will create more fullness, it will also shorten the length of the skirt, so additional fabric will be required for the hem. ▪ If a gown is too full at the first fitting, let it settle a bit. If it still feels full, ask the seamstress to remove a layer of net.

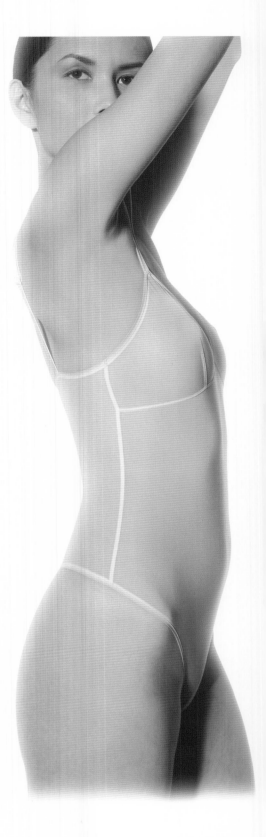

Because the choice of undergarment should be considered as it relates to the construction of the dress, it may not always be an elective decision. *Opposite* While a sheer, body-hugging foundation tends to be more modern and versatile, some brides, such as Camille Grammer, opt for a more traditional bridal underpinning.

THE WEDDING SLIPPER The wedding shoe should elongate the figure and serve as a decorative element in its own right. Shoes and stockings are central to the appearance and comfort of the bride on her wedding day.

HOSIERY When selecting hosiery, one of the most important considerations is matching the stockings to one's skin tone. ▪ The shade should also be determined by the shape and the overall condition of one's legs. For a thick calf, a darker shade will always be more flattering, while obvious scars or marks can be minimized with darker tones. ▪ The choice of hosiery should also be determined by the particulars of the wedding shoe and the fabric, color and texture of the attire. ▪ Specific wedding logistics such as climate and location will impact the texture, weight and weave of a stocking, as will the length of a hemline. ▪ While an opaque stocking is an appropriate weight for a winter wedding, it will add the appearance of volume to the lower leg. In warm climates, nothing is more sensual or refined than delicate silk stockings or ultra-sheer pantyhose. Be sure to buy several pairs. ▪ Regardless of weight, texture or color, any patterned hosiery is sure to emphasize less- than-perfect legs.

THE WEDDING LEG
A fundamental consideration

A FEW TIPS ▪ Pantyhose always provide a comfortable foundation and the cleanest line underneath a full ball skirt or a narrow, clingy gown. ▪ For a more elongating look, the hosiery should be the same tonalities as those of the shoes and gown. ▪ Pantyhose should always be worn with nothing underneath. ▪ Control-top pantyhose are a must for a full figure. ▪ Anything that bubbles or wrinkles will never work as a foundation garment. Even the slightest embellishment can be problematic: ribbon, lace or fancy trims are all visible under clothing. ▪ With impeccable grooming, bare legs can be appropriate in extremely hot weather. ▪ While white or ivory is symbolic of weddings, nude works with everything.

SHOES Even though the wedding shoe is rarely visible under a floor-length gown, it still represents an object of fetish and ceremony.

THE PUMP A beautiful pump is always appropriate. Even the most basic version can be instantly transformed into an evening slipper with the addition of a jeweled buckle, a beautiful bow, delicate embroidery or subtle beading. While lace shoes may seem like a great idea, they can be dowdy. Anyone determined to wear lace must find truly exceptional shoes. Any variation on a classic pump, such as Mary Jane's, ankle-straps or T-straps can be difficult to wear regardless of heel height.

THE SLING-BACK The sling-back, closed-toe pump is always a stylish choice for warm weather. Lighter and barer than classic pumps, high-heeled sling-backs are also extremely sexy.

THE SANDAL In warm climates, a beautifully jeweled evening sandal can be an enchanting alternative to a closed-toe shoe. In any heel height, a bare sandal adds an element of seduction to narrow gowns or full dresses.

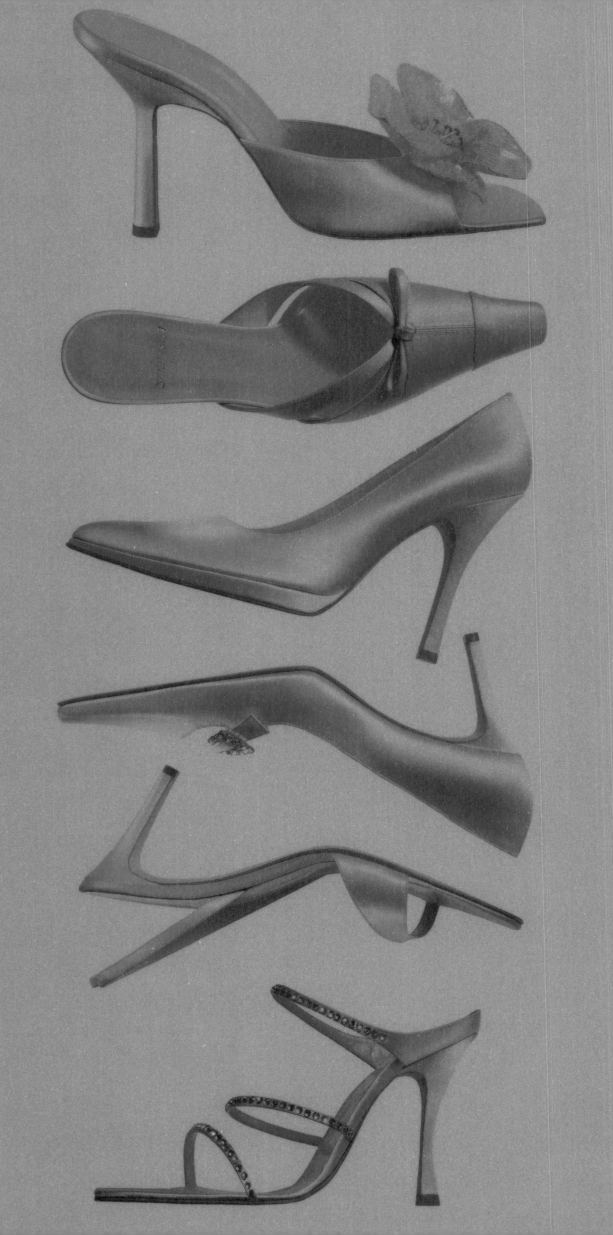

THE MULE For an informal ceremony or a more extreme fashion statement, a mule is an original choice for a wedding shoe. It is crucial, however, that the shoe feel secure, even if the ceremony is conducted in one's living room. Like a pump or sling-back, the *upper* of a mule provides enough space for fanciful decoration, making it an ideal silhouette for an evening wedding.

FABRICATION While satin dyes best, I also adore the elegance of silk crepe, faille and radzmere. For less formal weddings, silk shantung, linen, ultra-thin suede or leather can also be appropriate. Because white shoes reveal their workmanship, quality is important.

SOLES The more expensive the fabrication, the thinner and more delicate the sole. For brides who choose a full gown, I strongly recommend a subtle platform or a pump or sandal for added height. A high heel always feels more comfortable when balanced with a platform sole.

SOME TIPS ▪ Keep the heel height in mind when choosing a dress. ▪ Purchase the shoes after selecting the gown but prior to the first fitting. ▪ If possible, buy two pairs of shoes in case there is a dying mishap or one of the heels falls apart. ▪ Always consider the comfort factor, especially regarding toe shape and heel height. ▪ Be aware of what is flattering on your foot. For a size eight or larger, avoid a shoe with an extended toe. For a wide foot, opt for a gradual oval rather than a square toe. ▪ A plain elegant shoe or sandal looks infinitely more refined than one with garish decoration.

FOR A WEDDING, handbags, gloves and jewelry have practical functions beyond their decorative appeal. The most attractive combinations are skillfully orchestrated with the attire. Nothing detracts from a splendid gown like the wrong accessories.

ON GLOVES While gloves make a strong visual impact, I do not necessarily recommend them for everyone. They are often hard to wear and difficult to negotiate. That said, a pair of handmade, unlined, sixteen-button kid gloves can be extravagant and wonderfully sophisticated on the right bride.

ELEMENTS OF STYLE
Unessential basics

Above A group of unique handbags to accessorize every style of wedding gown. *Opposite* The luxury of paper-thin kidskin gloves provides a sophisticated counterpoint to the naiveté of a pink ballerina tulle wedding gown.

TIPS ■ Good leather or suede gloves are both costly and fragile. ■ Badly made gloves can make arms and fingers appear clumsy. ■ While stretch gloves fit beautifully, they do not always look expensive. ■ Gloves can be an elegant way of disguising some physical imperfections such as scars, discoloration or less than perfect arms. They may also emphasize heavy arms. ■ Always limit the amount of jewelry and other accessories when wearing gloves. ■ For a wedding, detachable sleeves may replace gloves.

REGARDING LENGTHS ■ The earlier the service, the shorter the glove. The more formal the wedding ceremony, the longer the glove. ■ As wrist-length gloves can look extremely youthful, use discretion. ■ For a morning service, a short glove with a subtle detail such as buttons, bows or piping can provide an elegant complement to an understated gown. ■ For an afternoon ceremony, elbow-length gloves can look quite sophisticated with a sleeveless sheath, a cocktail suit or a strapless gown. ■ The cut of a sleeve always impacts the

length of a glove. ■ If a standard length does not fit, a glove may be cut and reseamed. ■ The proportions of the glove should directly correspond to those of the bride. ■ Long gloves always create the illusion of height. ■ Long gloves look sensual next to bare skin, especially with a strapless or sleeveless wedding gown. ■ Long gloves necessitate incredible arms.

ON HANDBAGS A handbag should never be merely an afterthought. Since it is quite possibly one of the most difficult accessories to coordinate with the wedding ensemble, it requires special attention.

AS HANDBAGS ARE NEARLY IMPOSSIBLE TO DYE, when shopping, a swatch of the gown fabric should be kept available at all times. Like expensive shoes, an elegant handbag is an investment piece that could conceivably be put to use again. ■ Some accessory designers offer lines of shoes and bags that match. ■ With a tailored suit, the bag and shoes assume even more visual significance for a wedding. ■ Without exception, wedding handbags should always be small, elegant and refined. ■ Be sure to avoid excessive hardware and logos. ■ In ivory or white leather, quality is a must.

ON JEWELRY Where jewelry is concerned, less is usually better and infinitely more modern. While a few of my clients have based their entire wedding look on an important piece of jewelry, such as a necklace or tiara, for the vast majority of brides, a delicate pair of earrings, a string of pearls, a simple pendant or an elegant bracelet always works best.

SOME TIPS ■ Ornate gowns usually look dowdy with heavy jewelry. ■ Large jewelry can be distracting. ■ The neckline determines the necklace. ■ Jewelry should always be coordinated with the other bridal accessories. ■ The more diminutive the jewelry, the more youthful the look. ■ Do not mix jewelry styles or metal colors and finishes. ■ An unusual piece of jewelry, such as a brooch or pendant, personalizes a wedding gown. ■ A choker can age a young woman or flatter an older one. ■ Pearls are more demure than diamonds. ■ Place all jewelry in a secure place. Insurance is available by the day. ■ When wearing expensive jewelry, always be aware of your surroundings and those around you.

Above A pair of extraordinary wedding earrings with one white baroque pearl and one gray, circa 1930, by Louis Cartier.

SOMETHING OLD, SOMETHING NEW…

Mystery and magic

…SOMETHING BORROWED, SOMETHING BLUE
Where marriage is concerned, a bit of folklore
and superstition adds to the sense of adventure.
A delicate blue ribbon sewn into the hem of
a petticoat, a blue garter, a veil that has been
handed down from one's grandmother, a sapphire
necklace, a tiny handbound Bible or a delicate
platinum mesh change purse, all symbolize an
important connection with the past and the future.

HAIR Choosing an attractive hairstyle for the wedding is always a highly subjective decision. As with all beauty considerations, what appears in the mirror matters more than the current trends. The hairstyle needs to be determined before a veil or headpiece is selected. ▪ Like a veil or headpiece, a hairstyle should always correspond to the shape of a bride's face and her height. ▪ The ultimate goal for any bride is to look her personal best, not disguise herself beyond all recognition. ▪ An amazing haircut and a great blow dry will far surpass any contrived hairstyle. ▪ Be wary of hair extensions. ▪ Even with a vintage gown, choose a modern hairstyle. ▪ Tall brides should definitely avoid tall hairdos.

BEAUTY

Stay true to yourself

MAKEUP It may sound cliché, but the truth is, most brides are their most radiant when they look natural. The best makeup enhances — rather than masks — the woman wearing it. ▪ Avoid heavy makeup in daylight. ▪ A bright mouth looks incongruous behind a bridal veil. ▪ In daylight, the foundation should match one's skin tone. Blend makeup well to avoid a marked delineation below the neck. ▪ Day or night, avoid brightly colored eye shadows. ▪ Even waterproof mascara and eyeliner smear easily, so keep them light. ▪ For an afternoon wedding, makeup can be a bit stronger, though never artificial. ▪ For a young bride, a dark lip color with a matching bouquet can be a striking look. ▪ Create luminous-looking skin at night by choosing a foundation that is slightly paler than one's natural skin tone. ▪ Too much blusher or obvious contouring is extremely aging. ▪ Elaborate eye makeup suits a young bride best. ▪ Moisturize, moisturize, moisturize. ▪ For photographs, carry powder to minimize shine.

SPECIAL BEAUTY ISSUES Never sacrifice qualities of uniqueness. ▪ When wearing glasses, keep makeup simple. Lenses have a tendency to magnify. ▪ For girls with freckles, use a light foundation that evens out skin tone. ▪ If possible, keep your weight stable. Embarking on an Olympic training schedule during the engagement period can wreak havoc on a woman's health and sanity. ▪ Tattoos and body piercings should be kept hidden where possible. ▪ Avoid any cosmetic surgery for a year prior to the wedding. ▪ Maintain a natural skin tone.

Above A beautiful antique brooch fastened to the hair gives new meaning to the concept of jewelry. *Opposite* My friend Alberto Fava applying my makeup with his usual artistry.

WEDDING PREPARATIONS should include certain beauty treatments, some undertaken well in advance of the ceremony. The significance of a life-altering event such as one's wedding can wreak havoc on everything from one's skin to one's weight, so it is important that the bride dedicate sufficient time to prepare both mentally and physically for this enormous rite of passage. While many brides devote inordinate time and attention to their hair and makeup, nothing should take precedence over personal grooming. A polished appearance is the best complement to any gown.

THREE TO SIX MONTHS PRIOR ▪ Get a clean bill of health from your general physician or any specialists, plus all vaccinations necessary for the honeymoon. ▪ As nothing is more attractive than a healthy smile, take care of all dental related issues well in advance. Leave extra time if needed.

A MONTH PRIOR ▪ Conclude potentially irritating treatments such as facial peels or electrolysis. ▪ Have your hair trimmed, not cut. ▪ From here on in cease to experiment with any new beauty or health products.

GETTING READY
Figuratively and literally

Two of the most stylish brides I know, both exquisitely coiffed. *Above* Melissa Barrett Rhodes stepping into her gown at her parent's home before the wedding. *Opposite* Annette Roque Lauer getting zipped into her dress.

ONE TO TWO WEEKS PRIOR ▪ Attend final dress fittings. ▪ Schedule dress rehearsals for hair, makeup and veil. ▪ Purchase extra accessories like stockings and bras. ▪ Assemble your trousseau. ▪ Pack for your honeymoon. ▪ Have all necessary prescriptions filled. ▪ Start moisturizing. ▪ Get some sleep.

THE DAY BEFORE ▪ Lay out all clothing, including rehearsal dinner attire. ▪ Get a manicure and a pedicure. I prefer short nails in a pale shade of nude polish or a French manicure. This is not the time to make a nail statement. ▪ Apply a hypoallergenic moisturizing mask. Then moisturize again. Makeup looks best on smooth, hydrated skin. Use a product that will not cause an allergic reaction. ▪ If possible, get a massage. ▪ Spend a bit of time alone.

BEFORE THE WEDDING If you are not getting dressed at the ceremony venue, it is necessary to devise a strategy for the arrival, particularly for a voluminous gown. ▪ Have a steamer on hand in case of last minute wrinkles. ▪ Eat small, high-protein snacks all day, such as cheese, nuts, yogurt and peanut butter. ▪ For your complexion and your general state of health, be sure to drink enough water to stay hydrated. ▪ Allow extra time for everything, from hair and makeup to the wedding portraits. ▪ Once hair and makeup are done, put on the undergarments, unzip the gown and step into it. ▪ Drape a towel over the dress before any hair or makeup touch-ups. ▪ Dress in a separate room from everyone else. ▪ Once dressed, remain standing to avoid wrinkling. ▪ Once dressed, sip clear liquids through a straw to avoid stains. ▪ The headpiece, veil, blusher, jewelry and lip color should be put on last. ▪ Anchor the veil securely. ▪ Have the photographer on hand to document everything.

ON SCENT

A fragrance to remember

FRAGRANCE PROVOKES the senses and conjures memory in inexplicable ways. It also creates ambiance. For these reasons, it would be entirely remiss of me not to devote some part of my book to a bride's perfume. The significance of a fragrance that captures all of the emotion, dignity and sensuality of a wedding is immeasurable. WHETHER IT IS A PERSONAL favorite or a scent especially chosen to commemorate the occasion, a wedding fragrance is the most fragile adornment a bride can wear. Intimate and subtle, a bride's fragrance remains with her long after the ceremony is over. I wore my mother's perfume when I was married because I wanted to remember her. Even today, I treasure the memory.

FOR A MAN, a woman's fragrance evokes countless recollections: the memory of a first encounter, the scent of her skin on the beach, a lingering hint of her perfume. Her fragrance recalls all that is unique about her. Scent establishes a mysterious connection between time and feelings. Scent also deepens our imagination and intensifies our sensual awareness.

Portrait by Paolo Roversi

GENUINE INTIMACY, like sexual, emotional or intellectual compatibility, is one of those rare quirks of fate that can occur imperceptibly at the beginning of a relationship. It can also slip away just as easily later on. After the initial passion of new love, the decision to wed hopefully stems from a more rational confluence of reason and emotion. UNCERTAINTY CAN SPRING from any number of serious considerations – the enormity of a lifelong commitment, the staggering logistics of planning a wedding or the natural capacity for self-doubt. A deliberate effort is required to nurture closeness throughout the engagement.

ON INTIMACY

Privacy is the ultimate luxury

SOME SIMPLE SUGGESTIONS

WALKING The destination is unimportant. Taking a walk means carving out a bit of time for one another. Walking is a simple way of reconnecting and confiding. Early in a relationship, a quiet walk can be a prelude to romance. Walking still remains one of the most natural ways to create intimacy. During the frenzy of an engagement, it might provide the only opportunity to steal some time alone.

EATING It could be a hamburger in a diner, Chinese take-out at his place or scrambled eggs at home. There is an undeniable link between eating and intimacy. Any situation that interrupts the day's routine and allows time to share food and conversation provides the perfect escape. Whether it's a quiet lunch for two, drinks before joining others for dinner or cooking for each other, eating has always been a part of courtship.

BATHING Bathing presents an ideal occasion to experience a deeper kind of intimacy. Something about water sustains calmness and trust. In the privacy of the moment, words are not always necessary to express feelings. The tranquility of bathing encourages openness, relaxation and the inclination to connect.

Portrait by Paolo Roversi

THE SYMBOLISM OF FLOWERS

A definition of beauty

HAD I KNOWN MORE ABOUT FLOWERS and their inherent symbolism when I got married, my wedding celebration might have looked and felt so very different. Although white, long-stemmed roses were an appropriate but somewhat obvious choice for a formal wedding, there are so many other flowers I could also have used for a more personal experience. No matter what your preference, flowers can be a welcome aromatic addition and a creative tool for self-expression.

HERE IS A MEANINGFUL LIST:

Ambrosia	*love returned*	Lilac (white)	*youthful innocence*
Anemone	*expectation*	Lily	*majesty*
Apple blossoms	*hope, good fortune, better things to come*	Lily of the valley	*happiness*
Baby's breath	*innocence, pure heart*	Orange blossom	*purity, virginity*
Bluebell	*constancy*	Orchid	*rare beauty*
Blue violet	*faithfulness*	Queen Anne's lace	*trust*
Calla lily	*beauty*	Rose (red)	*love*
Camellia	*loveliness, gratitude*	Rose (yellow)	*friendship*
Daffodil	*regard, joy*	Rose (coral)	*desire*
Daisy	*gentleness, innocence*	Rose (peach)	*modesty*
Forget-me-not	*remembrance, true love*	Rose (dark pink)	*thankfulness*
Freesia	*innocence*	Rose (pale pink)	*grace*
Gardenia	*purity*	Rose (orange)	*fascination*
Heather	*future fortune*	Rose (white)	*innocence*
Heliotrope	*devotion, faithfulness*	Stephanotis	*marital happiness*
Hyacinth	*loveliness*	Tulip	*passion, love*
Iris	*warmth of affection*	Violet	*modesty, faithfulness*
Ivy	*fidelity*	Zinnia	*affection*

BY SEASON

Spring
Apple blossom, cherry blossom, daffodil, dogwood, forsythia, iris, jonquil, larkspur, lilac, lily, lily of the valley, peony, sweet pea, tulip, violet

Summer
Aster, calla lily, dahlia, daisy, geranium, hydrangea, larkspur, roses

Fall
Aster, chrysanthemum, dahlia, marigold, shasta daisy, zinnia

Year-round
Baby's breath, bachelor button, carnation, delphinium, gardenia, ivy, lily, orchid, rose, stephanotis

BIRTH MONTH FLOWERS

January	*carnation*
February	*violet*
March	*jonquil*
April	*sweet pea*
May	*lily of the valley*
June	*rose*
July	*larkspur*
August	*gladiolus*
September	*aster*
October	*calendula*
November	*chrysanthemum*
December	*narcissus*

THE PURCHASE Shopping for a wedding gown is one of the most memorable parts of the wedding experience. After all the excitement of the engagement, the quest for the right dress can provide a wonderful moment for a bride-to-be to bond with the significant women in her life. Nevertheless, where taste, style and budget are concerned, it may feel daunting to have to reconcile issues of self-perception, religion and wedding etiquette. Even well-meaning relatives and friends can add to the confusion. In the end, a wedding gown should fulfill the bride's own sense of identity. The purchase of a wedding gown is still a time-honored tradition that endures to day.

■ Determine the where, when and how of the wedding before looking at gowns. ■ Focus on silhouette during the first visit to a shop. ■ When possible, take along the necessary foundation garments. ■ If a special piece of jewelry, a favorite flower or an unusual color plays into the decision, bring those items or swatches along. ■ Do not purchase a gown based on anticipated weight loss. If there is a question about size, always go one bigger. A large dress can be taken in, but it is virtually impossible to let out a small one. Due to nerves, most brides tend to shed two to five pounds before a wedding. ■ Beware of buying a dress based solely on a photograph. Pictures are not necessarily reliable.

page 226

THE PURCHASE AND THE FITTINGS
Things a bride should know

■ The simpler the gown, the more precise the workmanship should be. ■ A grand wedding usually necessitates a more extravagant silhouette. ■ The longer the train, the bigger the bustle. ■ Vintage gowns are not easily fitted or repaired because the fabric is most often irreplaceable. ■ Wedding separates are a chic alternative to a gown and much less expensive. ■ Not every gown is right for every wedding.

SHOPPING The busiest time of year for bridal shopping is January through April. The busiest days for retailers are Friday afternoon, all day Saturday and, in some cases, Sunday. For extra attention, Monday is usually the best day to shop. DUE TO THE FRAGILITY of the gowns, most reputable retailers require that an appointment be made in advance with a sales consultant. Expect the appointment to last between forty-five and ninety minutes.

BE DIRECT with the dress consultant about one's budget. State the desired price range and be clear as to one's limits. A competent consultant can be of great help in advising on the purchase, but only if the consultant has a clear understanding of the client's budgetary parameters.

REMAIN OPEN-MINDED and receptive to new ideas. Many of my brides are amazed at their final decision. It is also important to allow plenty of time for the purchase of the dress. Typically, dresses take at least three months to come into the store, so if possible, begin the search eight to ten months before the wedding. ONE OF THE MOST IMPORTANT factors to consider about a retailer is the caliber of the seamstresses on staff. Only extremely competent technicians can manage both the specific and complex alterations that a wedding dress requires. CERTAIN UPSCALE DEPARTMENT stores have bridal departments. Some may even have individual shops dedicated to specific designers. Like wedding boutiques, they are equipped to handle most of the issues related to wedding attire: shoes, stockings, handbags, gloves, headpieces and veils. They can also ship and deliver anywhere. Another advantage of department stores is their revolving charge plans, but pay attention to the terms.

MANY BRIDAL RETAIL CHAINS buy dresses in bulk so they can afford to give discounts. While the shopping is rarely an upscale experience, it is possible to reap big savings if the right dress is available in the right size. Be careful of imperfections and defects.

WAREHOUSE DISCOUNTERS ALSO OFFER little in terms of service. They do provide the opportunity to see a wide variety of dresses. Most bridal houses and manufacturers have twice-yearly sample sales. It is, on occasion, possible to spend $1,200 for a dress that might have originally cost $7,000. Examine the clothes carefully for damage and do not expect alterations or returns.

TRUNK SHOWS ARE COLLECTIONS of a designer's most recent work. They are held all over the country, usually from Thursday through Sunday. Trunk shows feature the latest styles as well as gowns not necessarily offered in stores due to the price or the complexity of the design. This approach works best for the decisive shopper.

SOME BRIDAL DESIGNERS MAINTAIN their own retail establishments. I have found my shop to be an incredible way to stay in touch with clients and experiment with new ideas. I always showcase a dozen or so dresses that no one else carries.

SINCE VINTAGE DRESSES are one of a kind, they can be perfect for a bride who desires something truly unique. Be cautious when entrusting the design and execution of a dress to a seamstress. Alterations are one thing, but creating a dress from scratch is quite another. Made-to-order means made to one's specific measurements. This is a costly process that permits the bride an unprecedented level of control, since any detail can be modified or reworked to her specifications.

A HANDFUL OF EUROPEAN fashion houses maintain haute couture workrooms. Unlike made-to-order, these couture gowns are entirely handmade and decorated, and therefore require extensive labor, which is usually reflected in the price. Couture fashion houses do require a minimum of four fittings; there are very few haute couture clients in the world.

TERMS OF THE PURCHASE ▪ Once the gown is ordered, a dress order cancellation fee will usually apply. ▪ Fifty percent of a gown's cost is due upon placement of the order. It is usually nonrefundable. ▪ The balance is due upon completion of the dress, before the alterations are finished. Alterations are usually additional. ▪ In some instances, depending upon the retailer, the customer may be required to pay the entire cost up-front and keep the dress, no matter the outcome. Be sure to sign a Terms of Sale or Special Order Contract, with the specifics of the purchase noted.

THE FITTINGS The importance of fittings cannot be overestimated. For the beauty of her gown and her own peace of mind, a bride must devote serious time and effort toward fitting her gown. Regardless of its shape or construction, a wedding gown will only look beautiful if it is properly fit.

SOME VALUABLE TIPS ▪ Even an inexpensive gown can look elegant if it is properly fit. ▪ To avoid hemline discrepancies, a bride should bring her wedding shoes to every fitting. ▪ For uniformity of fit, always wear the same underpinnings. ▪ It is best to maintain a stable weight. Even a two-pound fluctuation can alter the fit of a bodice. A dress that has been overworked will look it. ▪ The initial fitting will determine the number of subsequent visits. ▪ A beautiful gown can be ruined by bad alterations. ▪ Most reputable, full-service bridal retailers are responsible for fitting the gown properly. ▪ Check with the retailer to understand its policies regarding alterations.

THE TROUSSEAU

Cashmere, cotton, silk and lace

IN THE PAST, A WOMAN BEGAN preparing her trousseau at an early age by sewing clothes in anticipation of her marriage. While the concept of a trousseau has little practical relevance today, shopping for the wedding night and the honeymoon is still an enduring wedding ritual. Whether it is a dozen bikinis for Bali, evening clothes for Paris or investment dressing for a new job, the implications are obvious: new clothes for a new life. BEFORE SHOPPING for the honeymoon, first determine the destination. Also, choose clothes that are versatile.

ALWAYS INCLUDE ▪ A lightweight cotton robe ▪ Cotton undershirts ▪ A cashmere twin set ▪ A little black dress with high-heeled sling-backs or sandals ▪ A trouser suit in a solid color ▪ A neutral-toned pashmina shawl ▪ Black leggings, for comfort, ease and practicality.

Opposite I love a wardrobe of pieces that feel luxurious when I'm staying in. Cashmere shorts, cotton tanks and little lace bras in sophisticated, flattering neutrals can represent a certain kind of investment dressing.

THE REGISTRY

As you see fit

WITH THE INSANITY OF PLANNING A wedding, registering for gifts may seem like yet another daunting task. The important idea to keep in mind is that the registry should reflect the couple's tastes and lifestyle. BEFORE THE BRIDE EVER GAZES upon a piece of Wedgwood or a Waring blender, the bride and groom should agree on two fundamental issues: where and for how long they plan to live in their first home. If the couple resides in different cities, it may be premature to register for a full china service or antique silver. If, however, the plan is to furnish a dream house, Baccarat crystal and monogrammed linens could be entirely appropriate and a necessary accoutrement.

Above A placesetting with a modern geometric border of platinum designed by Vera Wang™ for Wedgwood. *Opposite* A stemware collection in crystal created by Vera Wang™ for Wedgwood and inspired by an antique glass design.

FOR YOUNG COUPLES who bring few material belongings to a marriage, a wedding may be the only opportunity to acquire some extravagant possessions. For many, the compromise between everyday necessities and those special one-of-a-kind objects may seem difficult to achieve. These decisions, however, will impact a couple's lifestyle and the furnishing of their home.

■ Register for a variety of gifts within a range of price points. ■ It can be appropriate to have a group of friends participate in less traditional gifts, such as expensive electronics. ■ When registering for items such as china and crystal, be sure that the patterns are not discontinued. This covers eventual loss, breakage or any possible additions. ■ If possible, register with at least one nationwide chain that can service a wide variety of locations. ■ Register for specific items at alternative shops, such as a sports chain or a wine shop. For hobbies like cooking or gardening, there are home improvement chains and any number of highly specific catalogues. ■ For vacations or spas, there are great deals to be had through the airlines and online. ■ Even if it has little to do with furnishing a home, the wedding registry should reflect the personal interests of both the bride and groom. ■ Some guests may choose to refer to the wedding list for bridal shower gifts. If the registry is done early on, this can be a convenient and sensible way for friends to shop for other wedding-related gifts. ■ Registering is the perfect moment to complete a collection. ■ Some retailers offer a discount on anything left on the registry list after the wedding. ■ All gift suggestions should be discreetly conveyed through the maid or matron of honor. Wedding etiquette requires that no guidelines regarding wedding presents be written or spoken by the couple. Oddly enough, a couple's registry should never come directly from them. ■ Never use any gifts from the registry until after the wedding. ■ The only reason to return a gift is if the wedding is canceled. ■ For second marriages or couples who already have substantial lifestyles, it is appropriate to request that money be donated to charity in lieu of a gift. ■ In certain cultures it is permissible to give money to the newlyweds. Make sure this is acceptable etiquette given the cultural and ethnic background of the couple. ■ Keep all paperwork carefully organized in case of returns, breakage, errors or exchanges. ■ Write each thank-you note as the gift is received and recorded. Guests have up to a year to send a gift, and the recipients have the same amount of time to acknowledge it.

EVEN THE MOST UNDERSTATED CEREMONY involves a certain respect for ritual and pageantry, and no one plays more of a significant role than the bride's attendants. From the youngest flower girl to the maid of honor, they provide a prelude to the much anticipated coming of the bride. They also occupy a place of honor and trust throughout the celebration. LIKE EVERYONE ELSE, where attire is concerned, the bridesmaids, must take their cues from the bride. That being said, most brides today are increasingly sensitive to the tastes, feelings and finances of their attendants. If an occasion warrants a more extravagant gown, it is customary for the bride to assume the expenses. For less serious ceremonies, many bridesmaids are encouraged to select their own gowns, particularly if they reside out of town. Otherwise, there are less conventional brides who are entirely willing to leave the choice up to their attendants. While rules do exist, some brides choose to disregard them.

THE BRIDE'S ATTENDANTS

A few good women

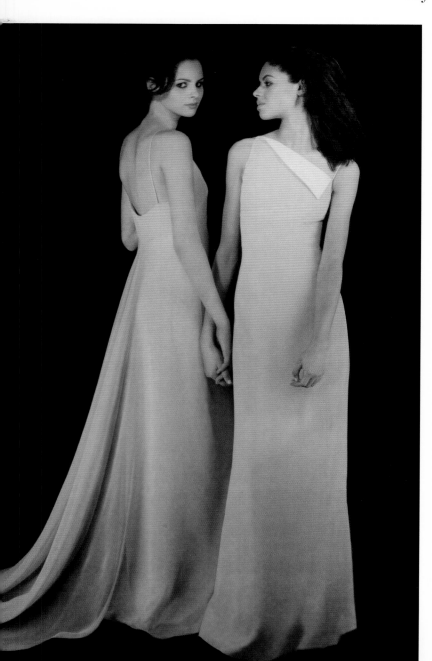

MATCHING ▪ For a traditional wedding, there should always be some degree of reference between the bride's gown and those of her attendants. ▪ Whatever the style of dress, it should flatter each woman equally. ▪ If everyone cannot wear the same silhouette, select different variations on a theme for each attendant. ▪ Uniformity of color, fabric, design and accessories can create a semblance of conformity. So can similar hairdos and makeup.

NONMATCHING Even if each attendant is choosing her own attire, she must still respect the bride's directives. By allowing each attendant to select her own gown, a bride is being inclusive, yet differentiating between each bridesmaid. FOR EXTREMELY LARGE bridal parties, conformity of dress can be somewhat tedious. On the other hand, each attendant in a different gown can be a bit distracting. Establish some common ground, with slight variations for each attendant: dresses in the same fabric but in different shapes; dresses in different colors but in the same style; all attendants in the same dress but carrying different flowers; all bridesmaids in the same skirts but with different tops.

Two of the most stunning and imaginative brides I have ever dressed, each with her own particular sense of style and invention. From the restaurant wedding of Greta Nicholas to the Greek Orthodox ceremony of Elena Fiveyskovo-Lollos, each celebration depicts a different variation on the ritual of marriage. *Opposite top* Greta Nicholas with her sister and matron of honor, Caroline Jerome. In this case, the bride did not wear black but her attendant did. *Above* Greta donning her veil for her marriage to Clement John Waldemann III in a private room upstairs at Raoul's. She is being helped by another attendant, Anne Waters-Grauso, who wears a white net sequined T-shirt and tuxedo trousers. February 12, 2001, 8pm, Raoul's, New York City. *Right* Elena Fiveyskovo-Lollos, a vision in a pink Duchess satin ball gown with bustier and chapel train. Attending her is her best friend, Olga Zemskaya, in a narrow bias cut column of silk charmeuse. The bride's maid is deliberately attired in ivory to offset the color of the bride's gown. September 8, 2000, 6pm, The Greek Orthodox Archdiocesan Cathedral of Holy Trinity, New York City.

ACCESSORIES ▪ Jewelry should always be minimal. ▪ For uniformity, it is best for a bride to purchase the attendants' jewelry herself. That way, the attendants might be less likely to object to wearing it. ▪ If the ceremony is religious, a bare dress must be covered with a shawl, wrap, knit cardigan or tiny bolero. ▪ Try to select a shoe that is flattering on everyone. Different heel heights can offset any height discrepancies. ▪ If the maid of honor is wearing an entirely different gown, it is also acceptable for her to wear a different shoe. ▪ It makes sense to choose one style of handbag for everyone.

GROOMING The same rules that apply to the bride apply to her attendants as well. ▪ Natural makeup looks best. ▪ Make sure everyone's hair is well-groomed, whatever the texture, cut or color. ▪ Hands and feet should be manicured and pedicured in a light natural color or a French manicure. ▪ Do not tan. ▪ Do not make any extreme or unusual beauty statements, such as body piercing or tattoos. ▪ If necessary, get a full leg, bikini and underarm wax.

STYLE CONSIDERATIONS ▪ A pale color can be subtle and more romantic for a summer wedding, while dark colors look great in winter. ▪ Any element of sophisticated color, such as a lavender sandal, a celadon pashmina or a deep blue bouquet, provides a wonderful accent for an all-white wedding. ▪ For an afternoon or evening ceremony, low backs or slightly décolleté necklines can be sexy and highly appropriate during summer months. Obvious cleavage, however, is never tasteful.

Opposite top right A bridesmaid with her own particular brand of style. Nothing could be more charming than pearls with classic, black canvas low tops. Even a traditional bridesmaid's gown can be totally updated. Hilary Tisch at the wedding of her father, Steve, to Jamie Tisch. Elsewhere, the bridesmaids adhere to the enduring tradition of matching gowns. Whether it is a party of three, four or twenty, there is something so completely correct about classic style.

LIKE THE GROOM, the groomsmen defer to the dress code preferred by the bride. While the season and temperature clearly impact the choice of fabric, the clothing options for the ushers are infinitely fewer than those for their female counterparts. Unless the groom decides to distinguish his own attire from that of his ushers, it is always correct to follow his cue. Although the best man has a unique role in the proceedings, stylistically speaking there should be little to differentiate him from the other groomsmen; uniformity is the goal. If designating the best man is a significant issue, though, a different tie or boutonniere creates some variety, however subtle. Pochettes that differ slightly in color are another way of distinguishing various members of the wedding procession.

THE GROOM AND THE USHERS
Men of distinction

DAYTIME DRESS

MORNING COAT OR CUTAWAY Less common than a tuxedo, especially in the United States, a morning suit is nonetheless a great justification for having a morning wedding. A cutaway is usually a wool coat in black, charcoal or light gray, with a single button at the waist and one broad tail in the back. It is customarily worn with striped trousers, a wing-collared shirt and an ascot of a different stripe. Sometimes a cutaway can be dressed down with a patterned tie in lieu of an ascot. A special touch is the bat-wing bow tie. Incredibly stylish but challenging to tie, it is an effective way to render a simple tie more special for a morning coat. If a wedding is too informal for such an important style statement, an elegant suit is a steadfast choice.

A SUIT A traditional suit consists of a jacket and matching trousers, any choice of dress shirt (preferably white) and either a tie or a bow tie. Again, the fabric is dictated by the style of the wedding and the season. Even for a traditional afternoon wedding, there is something wonderfully understated about a well-tailored suit. It can also be a suitable alternative to a tuxedo and a perfect foil for the bride's dress. For certain types of weddings, variations on a suit can be quite inventive. The key is in the nuances — the cut of a shirt, the width of a tie, the proportions of a collar or the curve of a lapel significantly affect the look of the groom and his attendants. For warm-weather weddings, my preference is a suit in classic seersucker or pale linen.

SPORTS JACKET, BLAZER For the majority of informal weddings, a navy or ivory tropical wool blazer is classic and effortless. It works best with gray flannels or khakis, a solid shirt and a classic tie. A variation on the navy blazer could be a houndstooth, plaid or herringbone jacket.

Above Waiting, willing and scared to death, my husband, Arthur Becker, just prior to our wedding ceremony, June 22, 1989, 6:30pm, The Pierre Hotel, New York City. *Opposite* Actor William Baldwin in a relaxed moment, at his wedding to Chynna Phillips, September 9, 1995, 11am, Southampton, New York.

LATE-DAY TO EVENING DRESS

WHITE TIE AND TAILS Tails are worn only for the most formal of evening weddings. The jacket is black wool, with two tails that fall to the knees in the back. The accompanying details are a white, starched-front dress shirt with a winged collar, a white vest and a white bow tie. This is still the most glamorous and debonair way of dressing for a man in the evening. Note: A woman accompanying a male guest must wear a long gown if the dress code on the invitation states white tie.

WHITE DINNER JACKET This can be a suave and sophisticated look for a formal summer wedding. Trousers are usually black or darkest navy. Otherwise, the rest of the attire is standard dinner jacket.

TUXEDO, DINNER JACKET, BLACK TIE A tuxedo is usually worn for formal late -afternoon or evening weddings. A version of a man's suit, a tuxedo consists of a single- or double-breasted jacket with satin or grosgrain lapels and a matching pair of trousers with a stripe down the side. The variations on a tuxedo are endless, from highly traditional to extremely fashion-forward.

Above Navy blazers and ivory flannels still cut dashing figures for the chic late-day wedding of Harriette and Peter Warren, June 23, 1994, 5:30pm, in the garden of her childhood home, St. Louis, Missouri. *Above right* Daniel Roberts takes a private moment at his wedding reception, May 22, 1997, 8pm, The Georgian Suite, New York City.

Above Haruko and Takayuki Kitano in a formal portrait after their wedding ceremony, June 1, 1997,
1:30pm, Tokyo, Japan. I adore the modernity of her wedding gown with the dignity of his kimono.

THE TRADITIONALIST ▪ A beautiful white cotton dress shirt with a bib of tailored pleats, tiny tucks or a panel of white cotton-pique waffle-weave fabric. ▪ A hand-tied black bow tie. ▪ A matching black, pleated cummerbund, worn with the pleats up. ▪ Dress studs and cuff links, instead of buttons. ▪ A pair of suspenders for added effect. ▪ A matching black vest, if desired. ▪ Black silk socks and black dress shoes.

TO DRESS DOWN A TUXEDO ▪ An all-black dress shirt with only the subtlest details and a collar that can be worn without a tie, such as a banded, Mandarin or Nehru collar. ▪ A dress shirt in navy or midnight blue. ▪ For a more festive ceremony, a matching bow tie and cummerbund in a bright color or a menswear pattern such as plaid, checks, dots, madras or a foulard print. ▪ Try to steer clear of tuxedos in shiny fabrics, strong colors, loud damasks or any unexpected combination of fabrics for the lapels and trim. ▪ A modern techno-fabric works well for the unconventional groom. Make certain the rest of the accoutrements are in keeping stylistically.

FOR RENTING ▪ Shop carefully. Investing in a tuxedo may be a wise decision, and fabulous deals are often possible at the end of a season. ▪ A rented tuxedo is more elegant with one's own dress shirt, cummerbund and bow tie. ▪ Insist on a great fabric, such as wool gabardine for winter or lightweight wool for the rest of the year. ▪ Trims should be low-key and tonal. ▪ A classic tuxedo always looks timeless.

OTHER SUGGESTIONS FOR DAY OR NIGHT ▪ A uniform conveys a sense of dignity and pride. If wearing one presents a possible alternative for the groom, it can be a unique and personal way to dress for the ceremony. ▪ Any native dress such as a Japanese kimono, a Nehru jacket or a Scottish kilt brings a personal and imaginative touch to the occasion.

CHILDREN BRING JOY to a wedding. Even if they panic, walk too fast or break down in tears, they always steal the show. They also imbue the solemnity of the ceremony with a sense of gaiety and fun. While children make a wedding celebratory, if there are none readily available, refrain from borrowing any solely for the sake of pageantry. As the wedding represents a moment of genuine feeling, authenticity is important. So is a love of children.

THE FLOWER GIRL AND THE RING BEARER Like every other detail of the wedding party, the flower girls' attire should assume some design element of the bride or bridesmaids' attire, whether it is a special decorative nuance or the actual fabric of the bride's dress.

THE CHILDREN

Charm personified

A FEW TIPS THAT COULD BE OF HELP
- The neckline of a flower girl's dress should always be modest. ▪ The ankle- or mid-calf hemline is an ideal length for a flower girl's dress because it is so manageable. ▪ For fall or winter weddings, a sleeve of any length is practical and age appropriate. The same applies to any orthodox or highly religious ceremony. ▪ While headpieces or hair ornaments are rarely worn today, they can be adorable on a flower girl. Consider a tailored bow or headband for a morning ceremony, wreaths of fresh flowers for an afternoon celebration or tiny rhinestone flowers on a barrette for an evening wedding. Delicate hair accessories are pretty as long as they are subtle. ▪ Shoes and stockings should blend in tone and texture. ▪ For a young flower girl in a summer or a warm-weather ceremony, thin white cotton socks look tailored, even with the fanciest party dress. ▪ If elegant white shoes are unavailable, satin or leather ballet slippers are easy to find and dye. ▪ For a finished look, young girls might wear short gloves. Plain white cotton always looks best. ▪ For little girls, the bouquet should be easy to maneuver. Complex floral arrangements seem out of place on anyone, particularly a small child.

Above Connor McNalley and my godson, Taylor Agisim, hanging out at my wedding. They look picture perfect in tiny tails and white tie. *Opposite* My daughters, Cecilia and Josephine, modeling my first collection of flower girl gowns.

THE ATTIRE OF THE RING BEARER, like that of the flower girl or junior bridesmaid, should reinforce the style of the ceremony. Though the ring bearer rarely carries the actual rings anymore, he is still an integral part of the wedding procession. Depending upon his age and physical characteristics, the ring bearer's attire should reflect that of the groom or complement the flower girls' dresses. If the ceremony is informal, a wool or seersucker blazer with flannel or khaki trousers is simple and tasteful. If the ceremony is formal, a dark blue suit with a white dress shirt and tie is an elegant alternative to a tuxedo. While a tuxedo on one boy may be fine, ivory cropped pants and a ruffled shirt may suit another. There is no rule except to maintain some common sense as to what looks appropriate.

Above left Vanessa Williams' son, Devin, is the epitome of style and elegance at his mother's wedding. *Above right* Haley Kimball Bloomer takes a break from her job as flower girl at the wedding of Alden and Emeril LaGasse. *Left* Bridgette Sampras poses for a portrait with her ring bearers, Adam and Zack West, after her wedding ceremony to Pete Sampras. *Opposite* Schuyler Samperton poses for a wedding kiss with her dog, Jack, and all of her attendants: Shelby Samperton, Corey Samperton, Reid Jewett and Jake Samperton. February 16, 1991, 6pm. *Following pages left* Harriette and Peter Warren's flower girls, Emily Moore and Annie Warren. *Right from top* Greta Nicholas and her flower girl, Kady Neill, in a banquet at Raoul's. *Middle* Corey Samperton getting dressed with the help of Debbie Brown. *Bottom left* Ring bearer Gideon Olshanksy.

EACH PARENT has his or her own distinct part to play. The most complex and challenging relationship, however, is often that of mother and daughter. Differences in style, vision and expectation can begin with the gown and end at the reception, with every issue in between fair game for controversy, particularly where finances are involved. A wedding can unleash torrents of emotion, and a bride must balance her own need for control with her mother's sense of involvement. Sometimes fashion can even become an excuse for unexpressed issues. DIFFICULTY can also arise between a bride-to-be and her prospective mother-in-law. The relationship between the "first lady" of a man's life and her successor may be fraught with tension. It is best to establish an open line of communication early on. Try to be sensitive to everyone concerned, as challenging as it may be.

ATTIRE Regarding issues of wedding attire, everyone must defer without exception to the bride. As they pertain to the mothers, however, if photographs are an artistic concern, there should be some visual correlation between their gowns and that of the bridal party. If this is not a primary consideration for the bride, the hour, season and venue should dictate the choice.

THE PARENTS
They hold a place of honor and privilege

- For a city wedding in a church or a synagogue, followed by a reception or a luncheon at a private club, a dress and coat or a cocktail dress with a cover-up can be stylish alternatives to a traditional suit. ■ For a country day wedding, a linen suit or a printed chiffon dress with a garden hat flatters a woman of any age. ■ For a formal, outdoor evening wedding, consider a floral printed georgette evening gown or a silk crepe column with a matching wrap and beautiful sandals. ■ For a formal hotel wedding, a crystal-beaded cocktail dress or a Duchess satin ball gown looks beautiful. If jewelry plays a role in the ensemble, choose a less adorned dress. ■ Always coordinate a wrap for the ceremony. The men's attire should have some uniformity with the other men in the wedding processional. But for variety, a special boutonniere might designate the father of the bride and the father of the groom.

Opposite My mother, Florence Wu Wang, my biggest champion, and me on my wedding day. I owe every wonderful thing in my life to her. *Left* My father, Cheng Ching Wang, comforting my husband-to-be with a little bit of humor and a lot of love.

THE STAFF

Last but not least

ALL DISCUSSIONS REGARDING staff attire and behavior should be addressed to the banquet manager, caterer, party planner or designer. Regardless of the venue, competent staff should always be present, never prominent. Unless costumes or special attire are to be provided, the more subdued the look, the better. For evening weddings, black is always appropriately unobtrusive. For an informal wedding, the options are limitless. Some possibilities are khaki or black trousers and a white shirt, a tailored T-shirt with matching trousers, or a white or black waiter's jacket with black trousers. Because performers are so visible during the reception, any clothing or style preferences should be expressed to the music provider well in advance.

A LIST OF POSSIBLE STAFF MEMBERS ▪ The floral and the decorative designers ▪ The party planner and the assistants ▪ The hairstylist and the makeup artist ▪ The dressers and the seamstress ▪ The security guards ▪ The waiters ▪ The bartenders, the buffet station attendants and the chefs ▪ The master or the mistress of ceremonies ▪ All of the performers — from the bandleader and the soloists to the musicians in the band or the orchestra ▪ The maître d', the captain and the co-captains.

Above right At Melissa Rivers' New York City wedding to John Endicott, every member of the staff was dressed in period costume.

THE DAY AFTER

Time to relax

WHEN HELD IN an unconventional venue, such as on a boat or at a seasonal resort, a wedding may become a prolonged affair with multiple festivities. For a treasured few or for those who have traveled a great distance to be there, a brunch or a casual luncheon is a special way of acknowledging guests on the day after the wedding. It also brings closure to such a significant rite of passage and serves as a gentle transition from the excitement of the wedding celebration to the relaxed intimacy of the honeymoon. Schedule the brunch at an hour that is leisurely and convenient for everyone. IF PLANNING an additional event seems too overwhelming, enlist the help of family members or close friends. Many couples wait a day before departing on their honeymoon. This can be a pleasant interlude in which to relax and unwind with friends. Ask the maid or matron of honor to help organize the remaining gifts, gift cards and any last-minute wedding presents in a safe place. Keep an index-card file of who was invited, in case they were unable to attend but have sent a gift.

THE ENGAGEMENT PARTY Usually hosted by either set of parents or a dear friend, the engagement party is less a request for gifts than a celebration of the forthcoming nuptials. It provides a festive atmosphere for introducing the families to each other, viewing the bride and groom together and having friends on both sides meet. Because some weddings are organized within a fairly short period of time — anywhere from three to six months — it may be difficult to negotiate everyone's schedules for a large engagement party. Some couples consider a co-ed bridal shower as a substitute for a formal engagement party. WHEN PLANNING a prewedding celebration, invite only those who will be included in the wedding. If a party is being held in honor of the bride and groom, the guest list should be carefully edited so the host will feel totally comfortable with the head count and the cost. If more than one friend offers to throw a party on their behalf, the couple should make every effort to accept. As with all wedding-related festivities, have a photographer present.

PREWEDDING CELEBRATIONS

Celebrating the celebration

THE BRIDAL SHOWER Bridal showers can be hosted by the maid or matron of honor, one or all of the bridesmaids or another close friend, but rarely a family member. ▪ Whereas guests may give lavish gifts for the engagement party, they are generally expected to give small and intimate gifts at the bridal shower. ▪ Invitations for the shower should be mailed after those for the wedding. ▪ Again, the guest list should be carefully reviewed and edited out of consideration for the hostess.

THE BRIDAL LUNCHEON It is a thoughtful gesture for the bride to host a party, whether it is a lunch, a brunch or a cocktail buffet, in honor of her bridesmaids and her maid or matron of honor. This celebration should provide the opportunity to present special keepsakes or gifts and personally acknowledge each attendant for her friendship and participation. UNLIKE THE BRIDAL SHOWER or an engagement party, where a bride must defer to her hostess, the bridal luncheon is entirely at her discretion. The schedules of all the attendants should be carefully considered to make the event leisurely for everyone. It can be held at any time, although it is probably most opportune two weeks prior to the wedding, when everyone is more likely to be around.

THE BACHELOR PARTY When I was a bride-to-be, my husband's inevitable bachelor party became an object of extreme scrutiny and anxiety for me. It was not that I feared a change of heart on his part or that he might be seduced by a bodacious lap dancer, so much as a feeling of uneasiness brought on by the fully sanctioned ritual of a groom celebrating his last moments of freedom unsupervised.

THE ONLY THING WORSE than my own paranoia was the thought of Arthur not having a bachelor party at all, as it represents such a special rite of passage. It is a privilege for a man to celebrate his loss of freedom with all of his best friends present. In reality, most bachelor parties are simply dinners with a lot of toasts and innuendo. The bride may offer to help the best man organize the celebration, should he need assistance.

THE REHEARSAL DINNER The rehearsal dinner is usually restricted to the bridal party and members of the immediate family. Historically, the rehearsal dinner follows the rehearsal on the eve of the wedding. It also presents a wonderful opportunity to include those who have traveled a long way to attend the celebration. Traditionally, the groom's family hosts the rehearsal dinner, though some couples choose to offer the party themselves. A rehearsal dinner is the perfect occasion for more personal toasts. ▪ Have a photographer or videographer present. ▪ If the wedding is intimate, the rehearsal dinner may include a larger circle of friends and family.

These pages Jamie and Steve Tisch's prewedding brunch on the croquet lawn at the Meadowood Resort, Napa Valley, California.

FOR OVER A DECADE, I have had the privilege of dressing some of the world's most celebrated women for their moments of public and professional validation as well as the most symbolic day of their lives. With the trust they place in me comes a tacit responsibility to create a gown that not only celebrates who they are but defines their true spirit. From the sweep of a veil to the curve of a bodice,

CELEBRITIES

Private moments, public faces

I'm involved with every nuance that surrounds the bride. This is the same energy and effort I devote to every gown I design. No detail ever goes unnoticed. SINCE MOST OF US are intrigued by public figures, their wedding day especially captures our imaginations. People always ask me what it is like to work with celebrities. When it comes to weddings, I have to say, they're a lot like the rest of us. All brides experience the same doubts, concerns and thoughts on beauty, style, etiquette and propriety. While discretion is always a given, where celebrities are concerned, it assumes a whole other level of significance.

AS THEIR PERSONAL lives are subject to such scrutiny, guarding their privacy has also been one of my primary responsibilities. For this reason, I am thrilled to be able to include a few intimate portraits of some of their most shining moments. I wish to share them with you for all the beauty, joy and emotion they express.

Left Ray Charles at Sharon Stone and Phil Bronstein's wedding reception, Valentine's Day, 1998, evening. *Opposite* Sharon Stone walking down the aisle in her living room, February 14, 1998, evening, Los Angeles, California. *Preceding pages* Chynna Phillips and William Baldwin, September 9, 1995, 3pm, at their wedding reception on the grounds of a private residence, Bridgehampton, New York.

Marisol and Rob Thomas on the lawn overlooking the vineyard, October 2, 1999, 6pm, Great Oaks Ranch, Santa Ynez, California. *Opposite* Heidi Klum and Ric Pipino leaving their ceremony, September 6, 1997, 4pm, Stoneridge, New York.

Left Liezl and Ernie Els on the portico after their wedding ceremony, December 31, 1998, 5:30pm, Stellenbosch, South Africa. *Middle* Amy and Judge Reinhold walking down the aisle, January 8, 2000, 2:45pm, All Souls Church, Scott, Arkansas. *Below* Ryan, Christian and Jaden Slater in a family portrait, February 12, 2000, 8pm, Four Seasons Hotel Los Angeles at Beverly Hills, Los Angeles, California. *Opposite* Bridgette and Pete Sampras at their wedding reception, September 30, 2000, 8pm, Los Angeles, California.

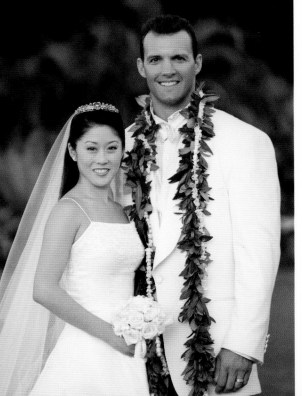

Opposite above left Alden and Emeril LaGasse at their wedding reception, the day after their ceremony, May 14, 2000, 10pm, Emeril's Restaurant, New Orleans, Louisiana. *Opposite above right* Camille and Kelsey Grammer celebrate their marriage at a private ranch, August 2, 1997, 7pm, Los Angeles, California. *Opposite below right* Lisa and Harry Hamlin on the dance floor, March 29, 1997, 9pm, Beverly Hills, California. *Opposite below left* Jamie and Steve Tisch cutting the cake. *Above* Leighanne and Brian Littrell dancing the night away at their reception, September 2, 2000, 11pm, Four Seasons Hotel, Atlanta, Georgia. *Left* Kristi Yamaguchi and Bret Hedican pose for a portrait on the lawn, The Orchid Hotel at Mauna Lani, July 8, 2000, 6:30pm, the Big Island of Hawaii.

Above Annette Roque Lauer and Matt Lauer, October 3, 1998, 9pm at a private residence, Water Mill, New York. *Right* Melissa Rivers and John Endicott, December 12, 1998, 9:30pm, Grand Ballroom, The Plaza Hotel, New York City. *Opposite* Victoria Beckham, July 4, 1999, 4pm, Luttrellstown Castle, Dublin, Ireland.

Above Tracy and Noah Wyle, May 6, 2000, 3:30pm, The Andrew Murray Vineyard, Los Olivos, California. *Opposite* Vanessa Williams and Rick Fox, September 26, 1999, 7pm, Grand Ballroom, The St. Regis Hotel, New York City.

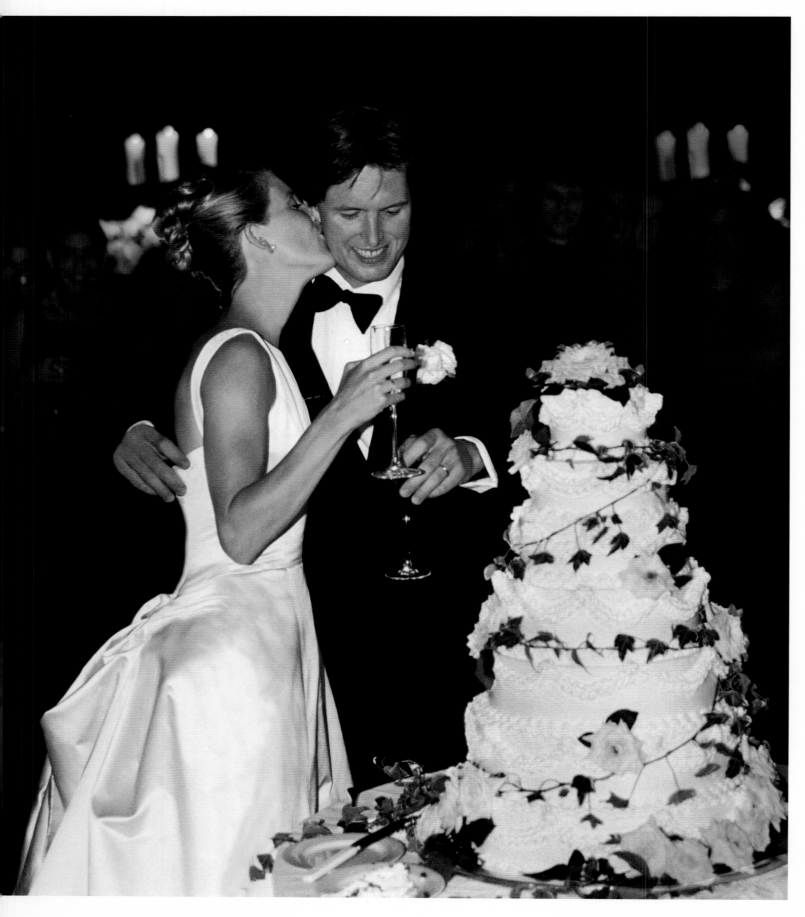

Above Karenna Gore Schiff and Drew Schiff at their wedding reception, July 12, 1997, 10pm, Vice President's residence, The Naval Observatory, Washington, District of Columbia. *Opposite* Vice President Al Gore escorting his daughter Karenna, July 12, 1997, 6:30pm, Washington National Cathedral, Washington, District of Columbia.

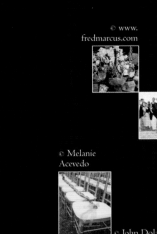

© www. fredmarcus.com

© Cyndy Warwick

© Melanie Acevedo

Lynne Brubaker; Ban Caribe represented by East Coast Entertainment, 800.277.6874

© John Dolan

© Yitzhak Dalal

All illustrations by Hervé Pierre and Adrienne Sugden for Vera Wang

© Julie Skarratt

© www.gruberphotographers.com; www.curtismusic.com 908.351.4321

© Mario Gomez

© James Wade

© Cyndy Warwick

© Julie Skarratt

© Krasner/Trebitz Photography

CREDITS

© Cyndy Warwick

Curtis Dahl

© Mario Gomez

© James Wade

© Krasner/Trebitz Photography

© Cyndy Warwick

© Kim Komenich; courtesy of Sharon Stone

© Michelle Litvin/Bill Stamets

© Harold Hechler Associates

© John Dolan

© Julie Skarratt

© Cyndy Warwick

© Cleo Sullivan

© Cyndy Warwick

© Mallory Samson; flowers by Glori Mundi, NYC 212.727.7020

photo by Paolo Rogerio; courtesy of Carolina Zapf.

© Denis Reggie

Photo courtesy of Yvonne Force Villareal

© www.fredmarcus.com

© Karen Odyniec

© Melanie Acevedo

© Lynne Brubaker; wedding coordinator Gail Hoerr

© Melanie Acevedo

© James Wade; sterling silver frames, vase, wine coaster & clock from Asprey & Garrard; stationery from Mrs. Strong; towels from Frette; napkins from E. Braun, NYC, silverware from Tiffany & Co.; wine from Sherry Lehman, NYC; large sterling silver frame from James Robinson Gallery, NYC; shoe by Vera Wang; stemware by Saint Louis

© Thibault Jeanson

© Lynne Brubaker; Bob Hardwick Sound, NYC 212.838.7521

© Julie Skarratt

© Thibault Jeanson

© Mario Gomez

© Melanie Acevedo

© Mallory Samson; flowers by LaFollia 415.391.0150

© Lynne Brubaker

© Callie Shell

© Amy Weber

© www.gruberphotographers.com

© Tanya Lawson

© James Wade

© Mia Matheson

© Genevieve DeManio

© Francesco Lagnese; flowers by Bloom, NYC; 212.620.5666; www.bloomflowers.com

© Melanie Acevedo

Mia Matheson; The Empire String Quartet, 917.312.6008, anoushsinonian@hotmail.com

© Cleo Sullivan

Mallory Samson

© Sean Gleason

© Mallory Samson

© Mallory Samson; flowers by Kira Gould

© Matthew Jordan Smith

© Melanie Acevedo

© James Wade; rings top to bottom: Kentshire Galleries, Bergdorf Goodman NYC; Kentshire Galleries, Bergdorf Goodman; NYC; Cartier; Tiffany & Co.; Tiffany & Co.; Fred Leighton, NYC

© James Wade; invitations by Mrs. Strong, Encore Designs and Anna Griffin

© Julie Skarratt

Photo by Kim Komenich; courtesy of Sharon Stone

© Tanya Lawson

Photo by Lillian Birnbaum; courtesy of Philippa Feigen Malkin

© Cyndy Warwick; cake by Chad zanzer Slice

© Julie Skarratt

Mario Gomez

© Sean Gleason

© Beth Herzhaft

© Thibault Jeanson

© John Dolan

© www.fredmarcus.com

© Cyndy Warwick

© Mia Matheson

© Tanya Lawson

© Krasner/Trebitz Photography

© John Dolan

© Denis Reggie

© Mario Gomez

© www.fredmarcus.com

© Yitzhak Dalal

© www.gruberphotographers.com

© Sean Gleason

© Julie Skarratt

© Julie Skarratt

© www.fredmarcus.com

Photo by Breton Littlehales; courtesy of Schuyler Samperton

© Mallory Samson; bouquet by La Follia 415.391.0150

© James Wade

© Tanya Lawson

© Sean Gleason

© Mia Matheson

Courtesy of Rachel DiCarlo

© Mallory Samson

© Sean Gleason

© Mario Gomez

Photo by Michael Keel; courtesy of Ron Ben-Israel; 212.625.3369, www.weddingcakes.com

© Michelle Litvin/Bill Stamets

© James Wade

© Mallory Samson

© Julie Skarratt

Photo by Lillian Birnbaum; courtesy of Philippa Feigen Malkin

© Sean Gleason

© John Dolan

© Morgan Tyler Photography

© James Wade; bag courtesy of Fred Leighton, NYC

© Krasner/Trebitz Photography

© Sean Gleason

© Mallory Samson

© Mallory Samson

© Julie Skarratt

© Cyndy Warwick

© Cyndy Warwick; flowers & decoration by Jody Perlberger of "Perl" 212.327.4470

© Mallory Samson; bouquet by Glori Mundi, NYC 212.727.7090

© Josephine Havlak; Battenburg lace napkins & table clothes provided by Party Arts, 314.781.1400; flowers by Ken Meisner, St. Louis, MO 314.567.6650

© Julie Skarratt

© Sean Gleason

Courtesy of Yvonne Force Villareal

© Karen Ochmiec; decor by Tansey Design Associates

© James Wade;
ring courtesy of Fred
Leighton, NYC

© Simone & Martin

Photo by
Mario Grauso;
courtesy of
Greta Nicholas

© James Wade

© Lynne Brubaker

© Mallory
Samson

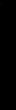

© Denis Reggie

© Victoria
Pearson

© Isabel
Lawrence;
Monterey
String Quartet
831.375.7270

© Julie Skarratt

© James Wade;
all stones
provided by
The William
Goldberg
Diamond
Corporation;
courtesy of
The Diamond
Information
Center

© Thibault
Jeanson

© Sean
Gleason

© John Dolan

©Abel Sanchez

© Mallory
Samson

Julie Skarratt

© Sean
Gleason

© Sister Moore

Julie Skarratt

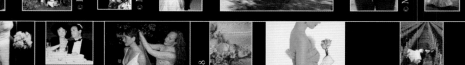

www.fredmarcus.com

© Lynne Brubaker

© Tanya
Lawson

Photo by Brian Aris;
courtesy of OK Magazine

© Mallory
Samson

© James Wade

© James Wade

© Victoria Pearson

© Thibault Jeanson

© Harold
Hechler
Associates

Photo by Kim
Komenich, courtesy
of Sharon Stone

© Gerard deLorme;
courtesy of Marcy Taub Wessel

© Cyndy
Warwick

© Melanie Acevedo

© Cyndy
Warwick

© Tanya
Lawson

© Tanya Lawson

© Cyndy
Warwick

© Lynne Brubaker

© Melanie
Acevedo

© James Wade

© Josephine Havlak

© Roxanne McCann

© Lynne Brubaker

© Melanie Acevedo

© John Dolan

© John Dolan

© Tanya
Lawson

© Mallory
Samson

© James Wade

© Tanya Lawson

Photo
courtesy of
Vera Wang

Photo by
Mario Grauso;
courtesy of Greta
Nicholas

© James Wade

© Meg Smith

© James Wade

© Mallory Samson

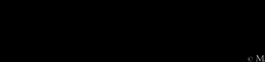

© Mallory Samson

© James Wade;
bags left to right
courtesy of:
Prada at
Barneys New York;
Larissa Barena at
Bergdorf Goodman;
Megan Park at
Barneys New York;
Barneys New York
private label;
Kate Spade;
Barneys New York
private label,
Prada at Barneys
New York

© Mallory Samson

© Mallory Samson;
cake design by
The Pastry Garden,
Poughkeepsie, NY
845.486.4255

© Cleo Sullivan

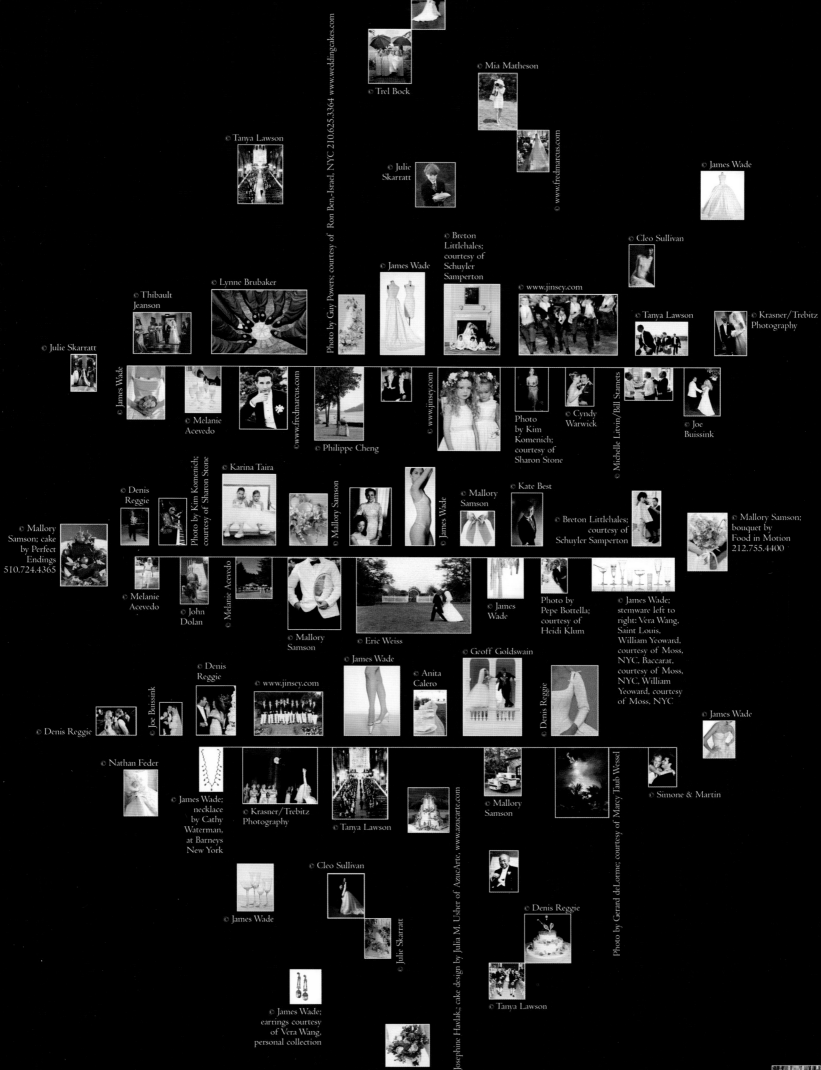

© Masa Tokuda

© Trel Bock

© Mia Matheson

© Tanya Lawson

© Julie Skarratt

© James Wade

Photo by Guy Powers; courtesy of Ron Ben-Israel, NYC 210.625.3364 www.weddingcakes.com

www.fredmarcus.com

© Breton Littlehales; courtesy of Schuyler Samperton

© Cleo Sullivan

© James Wade

© Lynne Brubaker

www.jinsey.com

© Tanya Lawson

© Krasner/Trebitz Photography

© Thibault Jeanson

© Julie Skarratt

© James Wade

© Melanie Acevedo

Photo by Guy Powers; courtesy of Ron Ben-Israel, NYC

© Philippe Cheng

www.jinsey.com

Photo by Kim Komenich; courtesy of Sharon Stone

© Cyndy Warwick

Michelle Litvin/Bill Stamets

© Joe Buissink

© Denis Reggie

Photo by Kim Komenich; courtesy of Sharon Stone

© Karina Taira

© Mallory Samson

© James Wade

© Mallory Samson

© Kate Best

© Breton Littlehales; courtesy of Schuyler Samperton

© Mallory Samson; bouquet by Food in Motion 212.755.4400

© Mallory Samson; cake by Perfect Endings 510.724.4365

© Melanie Acevedo

© John Dolan

© Melanie Acevedo

© Mallory Samson

© Eric Weiss

© James Wade

Photo by Pepe Bottella; courtesy of Heidi Klum

© James Wade; stemware left to right: Vera Wang, Saint Louis, William Yeoward, courtesy of Moss, NYC, Baccarat, courtesy of Moss, NYC, William Yeoward, courtesy of Moss, NYC

© Denis Reggie

© Joe Buissink

© Denis Reggie

www.jinsey.com

© James Wade

© Anita Calero

© Geoff Goldswain

© Denis Reggie

© James Wade

© Denis Reggie

© Nathan Feder

© James Wade; necklace by Cathy Waterman, at Barneys New York

© Krasner/Trebitz Photography

© Tanya Lawson

© Mallory Samson

Simone & Martin

Josephine Havlak; cake design by Julia M. Usher of AzucArte, www.azucarte.com

Photo by Gerard deLorme; courtesy of Marcy Taub Wessel

© Cleo Sullivan

© James Wade

© Julie Skarratt

© Denis Reggie

© Tanya Lawson

© James Wade; earrings courtesy of Vera Wang, personal collection

© Mallory Samson; bouquet by Caroline & Carrie Brown

© James Wade

www.fredmarcus.com

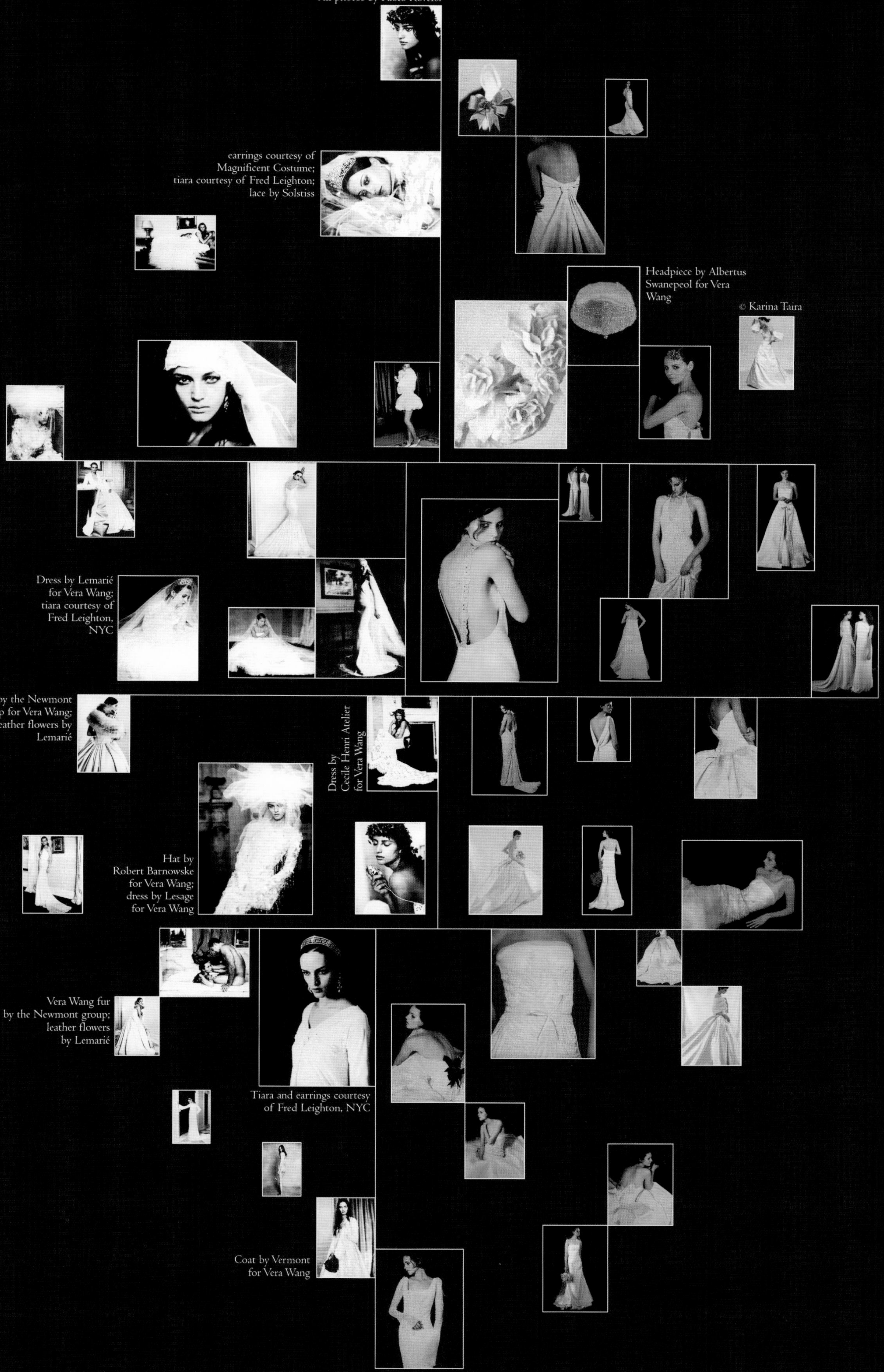

All photos by Paolo Roversi

earrings courtesy of
Magnificent Costume;
tiara courtesy of Fred Leighton;
lace by Solstiss

Headpiece by Albertus
Swanepeol for Vera
Wang

© Karina Taira

Dress by Lemarié
for Vera Wang;
tiara courtesy of
Fred Leighton,
NYC

Fur by the Newmont
Group for Vera Wang;
leather flowers by
Lemarié

Dress by
Cecile Henri Atelier
for Vera Wang

Hat by
Robert Barnowske
for Vera Wang;
dress by Lesage
for Vera Wang

Vera Wang fur
by the Newmont group;
leather flowers
by Lemarié

Tiara and earrings courtesy
of Fred Leighton, NYC

Coat by Vermont
for Vera Wang

All photos by Stacy Boge

PHOTOGRAPHERS

Acevedo, Melanie: c/o Elyse Connolly•212-255-0886

Best, Kate•212-864-4877

Birnbaum, Lillian: Paris, France•011-33-1-43-455-923

Boge, Stacy•212-686-6565•sboge1@earthlink.net

Botella, Pepe•305-674-7373•www.pepebotella.net

Brock, Trel•212-288-6120

Brubaker, Lynne•804-296-9376•www.lynnebrubaker.com

Buissink, Joe•310-360-0198•www.joebuissink.com

Calero, Anita•212-727-8949

Cheng, Philippe• 212-627-4262•www.philippecheng.com

Dahl, Curtis•818-708-7282•www.curtisdahl.com

Dalal, Yitzhak•323-654-6465•www.dalalphotography.com

Dauk, Jinsey•212-243-0652•www.jinsey.com

De Manio, Genevieve•617-524-1988•www.genevievedemanio.com

Dolan, John•212-462-2598•www.johndolan.com

Feder, Nathan•404-607-8499•877-902-9524•www.federgraphs.com

Gleason, Sean•212-462-4114•seangleason@earthlink.net

Goldswain, Geoff: South Africa•011-278-257-46788•geoff@goldswain.co3a

Gomez, Mario: Mexico•011-52-5-66-5-0485

Gruber, Terry•212-262-9777•www.gruberphotographers.com

Havlak, Josephine•314-962-8240•www.jhavlak.com

Hechler, Harold & Associates•212-472-6565

Herzhaft, Beth•323-653-2364•www.herzco.com/modernweddings

Jeanson, Thibault: c/o Bernstein&Andriulli•212-682-1490

Komenich, Kim•415-389-6869•www.kimkom.com

Krasner/Trebitz Photography•973-313-0792

Lagnese, Francesco•212-673-5735•lfstudiony@earthlink.net

Lawrence, Isabel•818-783-7252•www.isabellawrence.com

Lawson, Tanya•631-725-8233•tlphoto@aol.com

Litvin, Michelle and Bill Stamets•312-421-9040•www.michellelitvin.com

Marcus, Fred•212-873-5588•www.fredmarcus.com

Matheson, Mia•212-721-0808•www.miamatheson.com

McCann, Roxanne•310-456-6005

Moore, Sister•404-237-8727•sismoore@bellsouth.net

Odyniec, Karen•212-501-9221

Pearson, Victoria c/o Michelle Karpe•212-246-8555

Reggie, Denis•800-595-5253•404-873-804r80•www.denisreggie.com

Rogerio, Paolo: Portugal•011-35-121-917-5342

Samson, Mallory•212-673-0668•415-332-3697•www.mallorysamson.com

Sanchez, Abel: Golden Images•650-365-4230

Shell, Callie•202-483-2090

Simone&Martin•310-277-7717•www.workbook.com

Skarratt, Julie•212-877-2604

Smith, Matthew Jordan: c/o LVA Represents•212-541-4787
•www.matthewjordansmith.com

Sullivan, Cleo c/o Betty Wilson 212-502-0988

Taira, Karina: c/o Serge Thomas Photographers Consultant•212-260-8248

Tokuda, Masa: Japan•81-45-421-5486

Wade, James•212-255-1478•marcus.wade@rcn.com

Warwick, Cyndy•212-420-4760•www.warwickweddings.com

Weber, Amy•214-739-0711

Weiss, Eric•212-750-3921•www.eweiss@sohoweddings.com

The photographers listed here represent only those artists whose work appears in this book.

PHOTOGRAPHY AND VIDEOGRAPHY SUGGESTIONS

ANY OR ALL PREWEDDING RITUALS
the dress purchase and the final fitting
the veil purchase and the final adjustment
shopping for the trousseau

ALL PREWEDDING CELEBRATIONS
the engagement party
the bridal shower
the bridesmaids' luncheon
the rehearsal dinner
the bachelor party, if desired

THE WEDDING DAY
getting ready
everyone: the women, the men,
the attendants,
the parents, even the children
formal portraiture
the bride
the bride and the groom
the groom
the bride and her mother
the bride and her father
the bride and her attendants
the groom and his mother
the groom and his father
the groom and his ushers
the bride and groom with both sets of parents
the bride and groom and all of their attendants
the bride with her maid of honor
the groom with his best man
the bride's attendants
the groom's ushers
the children with the bride
the children with the groom

THE WEDDING RITUALS
the arrival of the bride and the bridal party
the arrival of the groom and the ushers
the processional
the attendants
the women
the men
the children
the flower girl
the ring bearer
the mother of the bride
the father of the bride
the bride
the mother of the groom
the father of the groom
the groom
any or all officiants
the choir or the musicians

the ceremony
the bride's attendants
the groom's ushers
the service
the exchanging of rings
the first kiss
the recessional
same as the processional
the signing of the marriage contract
the departure from the ceremony
the cocktail hour
the receiving line
specific guests and relatives
the special food chefs or servers
the musicians
the reception
the musicians
the first dance and the horah
the bride and the groom
the bride and her father
the groom and his mother
the bride and her father in law
the groom and his mother in law
the parents of the bride
the parents of the groom
the toasts
the cutting of the cake
the bouquet toss
the garter toss
the final departure

THE LOCATIONS
the venue for getting ready
the ceremony venue indoors
the wedding vehicle
the aisle
the seating
the altar
any special decorative effects
unfurling the runner
the ushers and specifically designated guests
the ceremony venue outdoors
the cocktail venue
special buffet tables
special cocktail tables and chairs
special decorative effects
the reception venue
the bridal party table
the guests' table
the stage and podium
the dance floor
the venue itself: walls, ceilings, doorway
special decorative effects

ANY OTHER DESIRED PHOTOS
the photographer photographed while photographing
the children getting dressed or dancing
close relatives
special toasts or speeches
a serenade at the table

TOUCHES
the invitation
the menu
the escort table and the place cards
the cocktails
the place settings
the party favors
the wedding cake
the bouquets
the wedding garter
the kitchen

WEDDING CALENDAR

SIX MONTHS IN ADVANCE

PICK the date, time of day and location.
WRITE the guest list.
DETERMINE the overall budget.
DECIDE which areas will get emphasis; food, flowers, lighting, etc.
BEGIN to organize every detail in a notebook or
with a software program.
SELECT the bridal attendants.
HIRE a bridal consultant.
BEGIN the dress search.
NOTIFY the newspaper.
ENGAGE a caterer.
SELECT the florist.
BOOK the venues for the ceremony and reception.
HIRE the photographer and videographer,
after considering these different formats for memorializing the occasion.
CHOOSE musicians for the ceremony and the reception.
GET a full physical examination, including a visit to the dentist and gynecologist.
DISCUSS feelings of religion and ideology.
GET any necessary blood tests.
SELECT the officiant.

FOUR MONTHS IN ADVANCE

PURCHASE all stationery: invitations,
announcements, thank-you cards, guest books, etc.
ORGANIZE the gift registry.
MAKE arrangements for the wedding night and the honeymoon.
BEGIN the trousseau shopping.
BUY the wedding ring.

TWO MONTHS IN ADVANCE

MEET with the caterer to finalize the menu and schedule a tasting.
DETERMINE the decoration details with the caterer, the party planner,
the florist and the lighting designer.
PLAN the service with the officiant. Discuss the type of vows, whether
traditional, original, or written by the couple.
SCHEDULE the next dress fitting.
ORGANIZE the rehearsal dinner.
MAIL the invitations.
ORDER the cake.

ONE MONTH IN ADVANCE

ORDER programs.
FILL OUT change-of-address notices at the post office, if applicable.
KEEP up to date with thank-you notes.

TWO WEEKS IN ADVANCE

GET the license.
ARRANGE the final dress fitting.
DETERMINE hair and makeup.
ORGANIZE the table plan one week in advance, if the
reception is a seated dinner.
CLARIFY all details with the caterer and florist.
CONFIRM any travel arrangements.
HAVE the dress delivered.

THE DAY BEFORE

CHECK in with the caterer to finalize
details such as seating and timing.
GET a manicure and pedicure.
WRITE a thank-you note to
each attendant.
HOST the rehearsal and rehearsal dinner.

THE WEDDING DAY

DESIGNATE someone like the maid of honor
to help the photographer identify important guests.
GIVE gifts and thank-you notes to the attendants.
MAIL announcements to those not invited to the wedding.

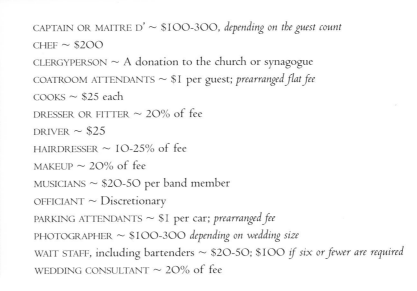

CAPTAIN OR MAITRE D' ~ $100-300, *depending on the guest count*

CHEF ~ $200

CLERGYPERSON ~ A donation to the church or synagogue

COATROOM ATTENDANTS ~ $1 per guest; *prearranged flat fee*

COOKS ~ $25 each

DRESSER OR FITTER ~ 20% of fee

DRIVER ~ $25

HAIRDRESSER ~ 10-25% of fee

MAKEUP ~ 20% of fee

MUSICIANS ~ $20-50 per band member

OFFICIANT ~ Discretionary

PARKING ATTENDANTS ~ $1 per car; *prearranged fee*

PHOTOGRAPHER ~ $100-300 *depending on wedding size*

WAIT STAFF, including bartenders ~ $20-50; $100 *if six or fewer are required*

WEDDING CONSULTANT ~ 20% of fee

TIPPING RECOMMENDATIONS

NECKLINES

HIGH

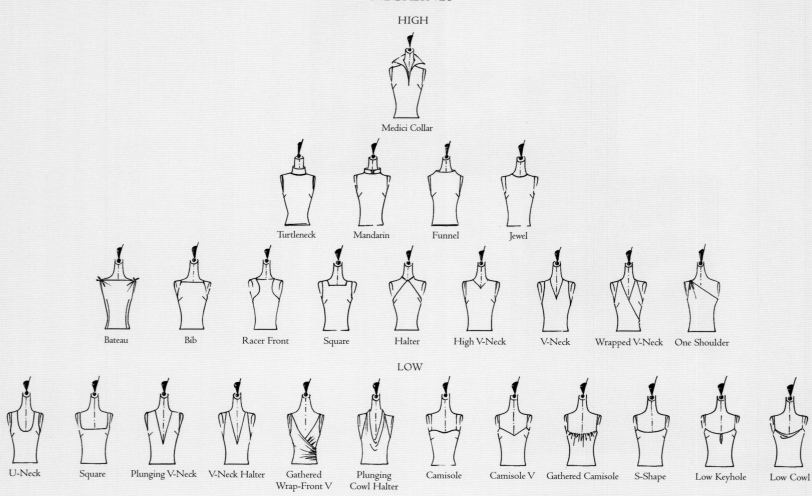

Medici Collar

Turtleneck Mandarin Funnel Jewel

Bateau Bib Racer Front Square Halter High V-Neck V-Neck Wrapped V-Neck One Shoulder

LOW

U-Neck Square Plunging V-Neck V-Neck Halter Gathered Wrap-Front V Plunging Cowl Halter Camisole Camisole V Gathered Camisole S-Shape Low Keyhole Low Cowl

SLEEVES

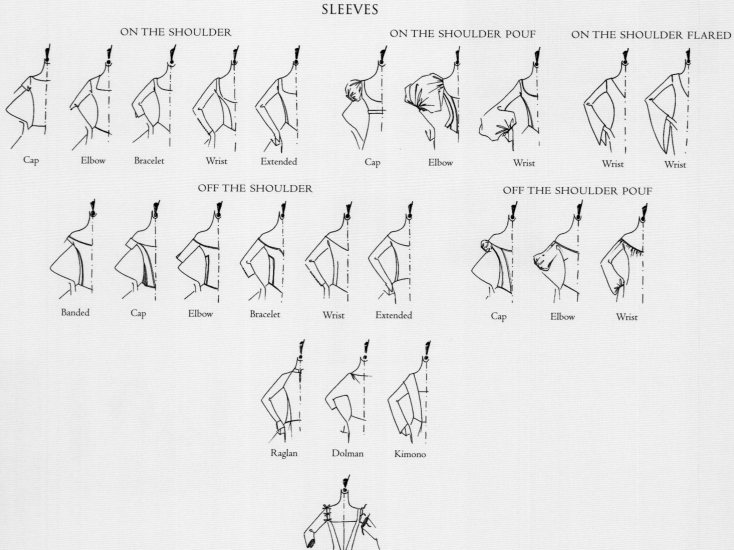

ON THE SHOULDER
Cap Elbow Bracelet Wrist Extended

ON THE SHOULDER POUF
Cap Elbow

ON THE SHOULDER FLARED
Wrist Wrist

Wrist

OFF THE SHOULDER
Banded Cap Elbow Bracelet Wrist Extended

OFF THE SHOULDER POUF
Cap Elbow Wrist

Raglan Dolman Kimono

Detachable

WAISTLINES

Empire Strapless

Empire Camisole

High Waisted Bib

Natural Waist Belted

Classic Basque

Scallop

S-Shape

Trapezoid

High To Low

Reverse Basque

Asymmetrical

Dropped Waist

Princess

SKIRT SHAPES

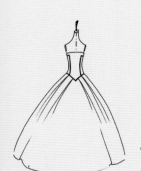

Classic Full

Full with Split Front

Full with Front Pleats

Full A-Line
Rigid Construction

Narrow A-Line
Rigid Construction

Narrow A-Line
Soft Construction

Circular
Rigid Construction

Circular
Soft Construction

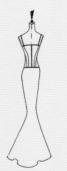

Mermaid
Rigid Construction

Mermaid
Soft Construction

Modified Mermaid

Narrow Column

Narrow Pegged

Dirndl

Full Balloon Back

Narrow to Full

SKIRT LENGTHS

Mini

Mini with Floor-Length Overskirt

Above the Knee

Below the Knee

Chanel

Mid-Calf Ballet

Ankle

Floor

Short to Long Rigid Construction

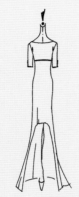

Short to Long Soft Construction

Asymmetrical

TRAINS

Watteau

Empire

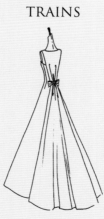

Natural

Classic Full Basque

Dropped Godet

Asymmetrical Drape

VEILS

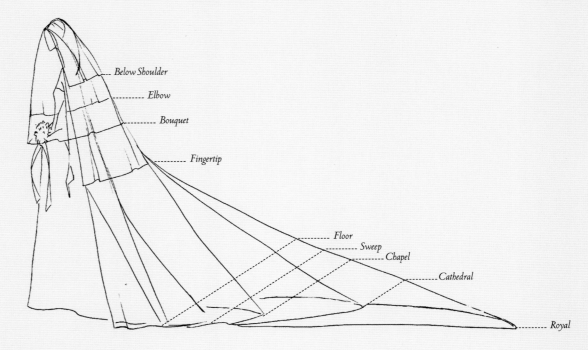

Below Shoulder
Elbow
Bouquet
Fingertip
Floor
Sweep
Chapel
Cathedral
Royal

DROPPED

Cage   Shoulder   Elbow   Bouquet   Fingertip

GATHERED

Cage   Shoulder   Elbow   Bouquet   Fingertip

Floor   Sweep   Chapel   Cathedral   Royal

BLUSHERS

Cage   Shoulder   Elbow   Bouquet   Fingertip

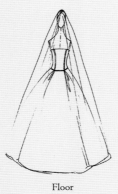

Floor

ACKNOWLEDGMENTS

I must begin by acknowledging my devoted family, whose love and support has shaped my entire existence and given it new meaning. I am ever grateful for their optimism and patience. To my husband, Arthur Becker, for his incomparable sense of humor, his intelligence and belief in me; to my beautiful daughters, Cecilia and Josephine, who endure Mom's insane work hours and inspire me everyday; to my father, Cheng Ching Wang, for whom I can never fully express all of my love and respect — his unwavering support, his concern for my emotional welfare, and his philosophical wisdom- have all influenced my life. And finally, to my mother, Florence Wu Wang, whose exceptional beauty, kindness, and courage guides me even today. Her personal style and passion for all things artistic helped to define my sense of aesthetics.

I would be remiss if I did not also recognize the many creative talents that I have had the privilege of collaborating with through my long career in fashion. As a senior fashion editor at *VOGUE*, for almost twenty years, I received an incredible education. They have been and continue to be a source of inspiration and influence. In particular, I want to extend my most heartfelt gratitude to Anna Wintour, for her friendship, support and advice over the years, and most importantly, her contribution to this endeavor.

Of course while this book reflects my passion for weddings, it also represents the extraordinary efforts of numerous other individuals, many of whom have dedicated the better part of three years to this work. A debt of gratitude is owed to them, for their tireless enthusiasm and belief in this project as well as their passion, loyalty and hard work. It wasn't always easy, but I hope everyone feels, as I do, that it was a great learning experience.

Firstly, to Polly Allen Mellen, my friend, mentor and collaborator. Polly was both a life force and the indispensable engine behind my vision for this project. Her singular work ethic and infallible eye were critical to the essence of this effort. To this book, she brought her unflagging taste level, legendary talent and experience. She was my conscience, my memory bank, my confidant. Polly's sense of modernity and her unique knowledge of women, fashion and style were instrumental in this book's completion, and continue to inspire me.

My heartfelt thanks to Bridget de Socio, for taking on the book's art direction at a pivotal moment in its evolution. A tenacious and tireless perfectionist, she showed the greatest resolve in addressing each and every artistic detail. Bridget was persistent in accepting nothing less than the highest level of quality and equally dogged in her devotion to the often difficult and time-consuming task of getting it right on a frequently demanding schedule. Her multi-faceted talents brought a comprehensiveness to the text and art that made this endeavor possible.

I also wish to express my gratitude to an artist whose work I have long admired. Paolo Roversi's extraordinary artistry and taste were essential to creating the sense of mystery and sensuality of women that I longed for. Paolo captured the beauty and emotion of passionate women in his breathtaking images of different brides.

Thanks go to James Wade for his wonderful still life and fashion detailing that enhanced the technical parts of the book. I would also like to extend my thanks to Stacy Boge for her contributions in the fashion chapters. Many thanks as well to all of the other photographers — over 125 — who submitted their work for consideration and use, and without whom this book would not have been feasible.

Chet Hazzard, my friend and business partner, is deserved of my utmost thanks for his tireless work and support of me and the business, since its inception. His business acumen, instincts and selflessness have been essential in helping me to realize my lifelong dream of becoming a designer.

My thanks as well to my publishers at HarperCollins, in particular, Adrian Zackheim and Harriet Bell, for believing in my vision for this book. I appreciate their patience and trust in me, and their respect for my personal insights on weddings and my passion for women, style and celebration. I am grateful to have been able to express my philosophy on my own terms.

I wish to acknowledge the others who worked so closely with me on this book. My book team, without whose efforts and devotion — to the project and moreover, me — were immeasurable; I am forever grateful. Halle Gaut, project manager from the beginning of the project, who personally reviewed the thousands of photographs of our brides from all corners of the world. Her dedication and unbreakable spirit will always endear me. I especially appreciate her sensitivity to and concern for our brides and their wedding photographs. She treated each one with the utmost respect, as if they were her very own. — Perhaps this is the appropriate moment to let our brides know that if you didn't get your film back in a reasonable period of time, it's because I had such difficulty letting go of the remarkable photographs; the invaluable input of Liz Gladfelter, my editorial manager on the project, who was faced with the nearly-impossible task of maintaining and overseeing order to my text. With great dedication, re-writes and edits too numerous to mention, she was always there: tireless and optimistic. To Robert Gerber, manuscript editor, who got me to cut down on adjectives and patiently helped me fine tune my thoughts. A special thanks also goes to the proofreaders who were engaged during the various iterations of this book.

I would especially like to thank the art and production team at Socio X, for their enthusiasm, perseverance and tremendous efforts on my behalf. Thank you for helping to create such a beautiful book: Malcolm Turk, imaging director, Christine Heslin, senior art director, Agnieszka Stachowicz, senior designer, Ilana Anger, production coordinator, Luz Jacome, Motoko Hada and Sung Hee Ham, designers, Eunice Gomes, digital imager and Gino Pazmino, Socio X's inexhaustible assistant. Without their devotion to Bridget, Polly and myself, the making of this book would not have been possible.

I could not conclude the acknowledgments for this book without mentioning the rest of my dedicated team: my designers, who work tirelessly to produce our many collections, as well as the couture featured on these pages. Their remarkable stamina and loyalty to the Vera Wang brand and vision is a treasure. As importantly, I am privileged to have an extraordinary atelier, who faithfully and arduously work into the night, transforming my designs into tangible visions. I have come to rely on their exacting eyes and dedication, as they work at my side, often for hours at a time, to perfect the drape and construction of my designs.

As with any company, without a strong business structure, it cannot succeed. I appreciate the immense support from all areas of our business, creative and financial. A big thanks to the financial, accounting, production, shipping and administration divisions, as well as human resources, sales and public relations. A special thanks to the retail network at our Madison Avenue flagship stores in New York City. Our consultants and those on our customer service and alterations teams are essential. On a daily basis, they dedicate themselves to pleasing and assisting our brides in making their wedding attire decisions.

Thanks also to the loyal network of exclusive retailers throughout the world who embrace and support our fashion vision. A special thanks to Barneys New York, for believing in our clothes from the very beginning. Many thanks for the friendship and support of Gene Pressman, Bonnie Pressman, Patti Miller and Michael Sharkey; a heartfelt thanks to Saks Fifth Avenue, for supporting our vision through the Vera Wang bridal salons at Saks Fifth Avenue. Other exclusive retailers I wish to thank: Saks Jandel, Washington D.C.; Suky Rosan, Ardmore, Pennsylvania; Louise Blum, Houston, Texas; Marcella's Boutique, Seattle, Washington; Hugo Nicholson, Toronto, Canada; The Wedding Shop, London, England; Liberty, London, England; and The Link, Singapore.

I would like to extend my personal thanks to Allen, Paul and Larry, of Grubman, Indursky and Schindler, P.C. Special thanks to our licensees, who supported this effort with their fine clothing and wares: Vera Wang footwear, Rossimoda; Vera Wang furs, Newmont Group; fragrance and beauty, Unilever Prestige; and Vera Wang china and crystal, Waterford Wedgwood.

My gratitude to all the designers and manufacturers who lent us the elegant merchandise that graces the pages of this book: Asprey & Garrard, Barneys New York, Bergdorf Goodman, Cartier, Cristal Saint-Louis, The Diamond Information Center, E. Braun, Fred Leighton, Frette, James Robinson Gallery, Harry Winston, Moss, Mrs. Strong, Neiman Marcus, Saks Fifth Avenue, Tiffany & Co., Waterford Wedgwood, Sylvia Weinstock and the William Goldberg Diamond Corporation.

I feel tremendous gratitude for my loyal clients, who continually support me with their enthusiasm and generosity. I cannot adequately express how it feels as a designer to see my creations come to life on so many beautiful women, who I have had the honor of dressing on their most personal day. A special thanks to Jodi Della Femina, and all of our brides who submitted their photographs for consideration and use in the book. We treasured each and every picture and were sorry we could not use them all.

My deepest appreciation and love to Sharon Stone and Phil Bronstein, who have never before released their wedding photos to the public. And, last but not least, thank you: Victoria Beckham, Liezl Els, Mary Joe Fernandez, Camille Grammer, Lisa Hamlin, Heidi Klum, Alden LaGasse, Annette Roque Lauer, Leighanne Littrell, Chynna Phillips, Amy Reinhold, Melissa Rivers, Bridgette Sampras, Karenna Gore Schiff, Ryan Haddon Slater, Marisol Thomas, Vanessa Williams, Tracy Wyle and Kristi Yamaguchi.